Essays in Linguistics

Essays in Linguistics

By

JOSEPH H. GREENBERG

Phoenix Books

THE UNIVERSITY OF CHICAGO PRESS

This volume has also been issued by the Wenner-Gren Foundation for Anthropological Research, Incorporated, as *Viking Fund Publications in Anthropology Number 24*, in a limited, paper-bound edition for private distribution to scholars and institutions throughout the world. The publishers gratefully acknowledge the permission granted by the Foundation for the appearance of this edition.

This book is also available in a clothbound edition from

THE UNIVERSITY OF CHICAGO PRESS

Library of Congress Catalog Card Number: 57-6273

THE UNIVERSITY OF CHICAGO PRESS, CHICAGO & LONDON
The University of Toronto Press, Toronto 5, Canada

PREFACE

THE essays of this collection are intended as separate treatments of a number of topics in linguistics. They fall quite naturally into three groups, the first two being concerned with the methodology of language description, the third and fourth with historical linguistics, and the remaining four with the relation between language and culture. Though not designed to cover the entire field of linguistics, almost every topic comes in for some discussion. The most serious omissions are the absence of any treatment of phonemic theory and of any over-all discussion of meaning, though semantic problems are touched on incidentally at several points.

There are obvious interconnections among the ideas expressed in some of the essays, though they are not meant to present any coherent "system." In the nature of things, problems as diverse as those dealt with here often have solutions which do not depend on one another. If there is any single point of view that runs through the whole, it is that further substantial progress in linguistics requires the abandonment of its traditional isolationism, one for which there was formerly much justification, in favor of a willingness to explore connections in other directions. The borderline areas most prominent in the present essays are those with logic, mathematics, anthropology, and psychology, but, of course, others exist.

I have written chiefly for those anthropologists, in whatever branch of the subject they are engaged, who, because of their interest in cultural theory, are aware of the significance of so fundamental a human trait as language to any general science of man. The essays are reasonably independent of one another, and the less linguistically oriented anthropologist who finds the first two essays in particular somewhat technical and remote from his main interests should have no compunction in passing them by. On the other hand, these may well be precisely the essays which hold the most real interest for the logician or mathematician interested in the possibility of a general syntax, of which linguistics would be but a branch. The mathematical reader should bear in mind that my own command of mathematics is very far from professional, and, in view of the purposes of the essays as a whole, I have not assumed any but an elementary acquaintance with mathematics on the part of the reader. For this reason also, a few topics of more purely mathematical interest have been relegated to appendixes.

None of the essays has appeared elsewhere in its present form. However, the essay "Genetic Relationship among Languages" is an expanded and revised version of "Historical Linguistics and Unwritten Languages," which appeared in *Anthropology Today*, edited by A. L. Kroeber (Chicago, 1952), pages 265–87; and parts of the discussion of the definition of the word and the morpheme occur in an article entitled "A Quantitative Approach to the Morphological Typology of Language," in *Methods and Perspectives in Anthropology: Papers in Honor of Wilson D. Wallis*, edited by Robert F. Spencer (Minneapolis, 1954), and in *Psycholinguistics: A Survey of Theory and Research Problems* (Baltimore, 1954). "Language and Evolutionary Theory" was the topic of a talk at the Wenner-Gren Foundation in 1951, and the subject matters of "Order of Affixing" and "Language as a Sign System" were discussed in talks at Michigan and Yale, respectively, in 1954. On all these occasions, I derived benefit from oral comments and criticisms.

I am grateful to the Ford Foundation, which provided the necessary leisure, under a Faculty Research Fellowship, to pursue my interest in logic and mathematics and to write the essays as a whole. I am also in the debt of the Social Science Research Council for the opportunity to participate in its summer seminar of 1953 in psycholinguistics at the University of Indiana, at which some of the ideas regarding the definition of the word were first developed and presented in oral discussion and which also stimulated my interest in the connection between language universals and general psychology, which figures in the final essay.

The first version of these essays was written during the summer of 1954, and no systematic account is taken of the literature which has appeared since that time.

I am indebted to Professor Marvin Harris for observations regarding the difference between scientific and ordinary language, which helped to orient my thinking in the area of language and evolution, and to Professors Charles Osgood and Floyd Lounsbury, whose discussion of psychological learning theory in relation to prefixing and suffixing provided the initial stimulus for the essay on the order of affixed elements.

Finally, and by no means least, I owe a debt of gratitude to my wife Selma for her sympathetic understanding during the period I was writing these essays.

JOSEPH H. GREENBERG

TABLE OF CONTENTS

CHAPTER I

LANGUAGE AS A SIGN SYSTEM

LANGUAGE can be approached in either of two ways: as a system of signals conforming to the rules which constitute its grammar or as a set of culturally transmitted behavior patterns shared by a group of individuals. It is the first of these aspects that will interest us for the present; but in later chapters of this work language as the heritage of cultural groups will receive a major share of attention.

As a system, it is natural to compare spoken language with other forms which likewise consist of ordered arrays of elements in some physical medium and obey fixed rules of combination. For example, the expressions of mathematics seem to display a certain analogy with language. From a limited number of elementary symbols, sequences of finite length are built in conformity with certain rules which may be called the "grammar" of the system. A general discipline whose subject matter embraces such systems would contain the study of linguistic systems as a subdivision. In this way the analytical problems of language might be put into the broader perspective of a semiotic whose terminology would apply equally to linguistic and to non-linguistic systems.

Such a branch of inquiry belongs to the logico-mathematical group of studies, since it will consider the nature of all possible systems with postulated characteristics. Even its linguistic subdivision will be distinct from, though in intimate relation with, linguistics, which remains an empirical social science dealing with the description, history, and ethnolinguistics of actually existing languages.

Our first task will be to establish more precisely than has been possible in these few preliminary remarks the defining characteristics of the systems to be included in such a general semiotic. The well-known distinction among three aspects of sign behavior—the syntactic, the semantic, and the pragmatic—introduced by Charles W. Morris will serve as a convenient point of departure.[1] This analysis starts from the sign situation as involving three factors—the sign itself, the referent, and the organism who produces or reacts to the sign. The syntactic aspect is one in which only the relation of sign to sign is included, abstractions being made of both the referent and the organism. In the semantic aspect the relation between sign and referent is taken into account, but the organism is excluded. In the pragmatic aspect, all three—the organism, the sign, and the referent—are taken into consideration. The pragmatic aspect is usually understood as treating of the actual behavior of organisms in their use of the sign system as opposed to the rules of the sign system

1. In his *Foundations of the Theory of Signs* (*International Encyclopedia of Unified Science*, Vol. I, No. 2 [Chicago, 1935]).

viewed as a calculus without regard to meaning, which is the subject matter of syntactics, and to the meanings which belong to semantics.

If we direct our attention to semantics for a moment, however, it can be seen that a distinction can be made within semantics analogous to that between syntactics and pragmatics. We have, on the one hand, semantic rules, rules of meaning, and, on the other hand, the actual behavior of organisms in regard to meaning in their use of the language. The former is a kind of syntactic-semantics, the latter a pragmatic-semantics. If we turn now to the sign as a physical object, a similar differentiation can be made between the rule which specifies which physical phenomena shall be instances of a particular sign vehicle and the actual behavior of sign-using organisms in this regard. The same distinction also holds between rules of sign arrangement and actual behavior in regard to sign arrangement. To avoid confusion with the technical use of the term "syntax" in language, we may call "systemic" those investigations having to do with the formulation and discovery of rules and retain the term "pragmatic" to refer to the behavior of organisms in their use of systems. To designate rules concerning the arrangements of signs without regard to meaning, the term "grammar" may be extended from its employment in linguistics to cover sign systems in general. This results in six aspects of sign systems, as indicated in the accompanying table. Then linguistics is concerned with

	Systemic	Pragmatic
Physical	*Linguistics*	*Social sciences*
Semantic		
Grammatical		

the systemic aspects of a particular group of actually existing sign systems, the so-called "natural languages," while psychology and the social sciences, in so far as they deal with verbal behavior, consider the pragmatic aspects of these same systems. Although it was not drawn up with this purpose in view, the present analysis tends to justify the traditional division of language descriptions into phonology (the physical aspect), lexicography (the semantic aspect), and grammar (the grammatical aspect).

Confining ourselves henceforth to the realm of the systemic, we can see that, of the three aspects—the physical, the semantic, and the grammatical—not all are equally indispensable. It is possible to have systems of elements subject to certain specified rules of arrangements but without any meanings assigned to the elements. Such a system will have physical and grammatical, but no semantic, rules. A system which lacks semantic rules may be called a "calculus" or an "uninterpreted system." Systems which include rules of meaning will be called "interpreted systems."

A further distinction may be made between systems, here called "specified," in which the nature of the physical objects which are to function as the actual signs is specified by rules, and abstract systems, in which it is not.[2] The physical aspect

2. The use of the term "abstract" here corresponds to its employment in group theory where groups with different elements but the same structure, and hence connected by one-to-one isomorphisms, are said to represent the same abstract group.

is thus also dispensable. The various specified systems which are realizations of the same abstract system are connected by a relation of isomorphism. A common example of isomorphic systems is a spoken language and its written form in phonemic transcription. For an isomorphism to exist, we must have a set of one-to-one transformations of the two systems which carries every expression of one language into its corresponding expression in the other. The monoalphabetic substitution ciphers of the Sunday supplement cryptograms are examples of systems isomorphically related to written English by element-for-element substitution rules.

The grammatical aspect alone is indispensable. There can be no system without rules of arrangement. As an inclusive designation for all systems, whether calculi or interpreted systems, whether specified or abstract, the term "sign system" will be used (hereafter abbreviated to "SS").[3] As a logical minimum for a sign system, we require a set of elements, whether specified or not, ordered into sequences called "expressions" by a serial relation and conforming to definite rules of combination. The number of elements may be finite or infinite.[4] The number of expressions may likewise be finite or infinite. A system will be called "finite" or "infinite," respectively, depending on whether the number of its expressions is finite or infinite. The basic serial relation of a sign system, if specified, must be defined along with the physical shape of its elements. We take the ordering in time of the elements of spoken language so for granted that this tends to be forgotten. As soon as we specify an isomorphic system in the visual medium of writing, we see that a direction, whether from left to right, from right to left, or downward, etc., must be defined as the isomorphic substitute of the relation "following in time." In addition to the basic serial relation, a system may have others. In language, sentence intonations, which are in relation to an expression as a whole, furnish an example. In mathematics the relation between a numeral on the line and a power written above and to the right is an additional relation. Thus 34 and 3^4 contain the same elements connected by different relations. A more rigorous statement of the requirement of a single serial relation, as well as a discussion of types of systems generated by additional relations, is to be found in Appendix I, "On Basic Relations in Sign Systems."

Two specified systems whose elements are identical if equal in number, or such that all the elements of the system with the smaller number of elements are identical with some elements in the larger system, are said to be "homogeneous"; otherwise, "heterogeneous." Written English and written French are homogeneous. Written English and written Russian are heterogeneous. The element order of a system

3. This term is inappropriate, since a sign is generally thought of as having some meaning, but no term that will express exactly what is wanted seems available.

4. An example of a system with an infinite number of elements would be one in which the first sign consisted of one vertical line to which were added, perpendicularly on the right, up to, say, five horizontal lines. When this was reached, the next sign would add a vertical line perpendicular to the preceding five horizontal lines. To it, in turn, would be added up to five vertical lines, and so on. A construction in this SS might be limited to a sequence of any two signs of the system. In this case there would be an infinite number of expressions in the system, even though two was the maximum length of any expression.

is the number of elements it contains. Written English has the element order 26. Sometimes, when there is no risk of confusion with the term "sequence order," to be introduced later, this will be called merely "order."

Certain concepts and notations drawn from the mathematical theory of sets or aggregates will prove useful.[5] An SS will be considered a set whose members are the expressions of the system. One SS will be said to be equal to another if both contain the same expressions, in symbols, $M_1 = M_2$. If all the expressions of M_1 are also expressions of M_2 but not all the expressions of M_2 are expressions of M_1, then M_1 is contained in, or is a proper part of, M_2 ($M_1 \subset M_2$). If all the expressions of M_1 are expressions of M_2, then M_1 is equal to, or is contained in, M_2 ($M_1 \subseteq M_2$). The system which contains all the expressions of M_1 and all the expressions of M_2, including those found in both, is called the "union" of M_1 and M_2 ($M_1 \cup M_2$). The system which contains only those expressions which are in both M_1 and M_2 is the intersection of these two systems, $M_1 \cap M_2$. For all homogeneous systems of the same order there is one SS in which all the others are contained. This SS, indicated by I^n, where n indicates the order, is simply the unrestricted set of permutations and combinations of the n symbols and will be called the "infinite system" of that order.

For example, I^4, with symbols specified as a, b, c, and d, has four expressions of length (hereafter abbreviated l) 1: a, b, c, d, and sixteen expressions for $l = 2$: aa, ab, ac, ad, ba, bb, bc, bd, ca, cb, cc, cd, da, db, dc, dd. In fact, the number of expressions in I^n of length l is l^n. The unrestricted set of permutations and combinations in an SS with an infinite number of elements, I^∞, contains every homogeneous SS of whatever order. In general, if $m < n$, then I^n contains every homogeneous SS of order m.

For every order we have an ideal construction, the null system, which contains no expressions and which corresponds to the empty set. It will be indicated by 0^n. $M_1 - M_2$ indicates the SS which has all those expressions which are in M_1 but not in M_2. To every system M_1, there corresponds another system $-M_1$, called its "complement," consisting only of those homogeneous expressions of the same order which are not members of M_1. This system may be defined as $I - M_1$.

The isomorphism of the set of all homogeneous SS of order $\leq n$ to the algebra of classes is obvious. In fact, it forms a Boolean algebra of an infinite number of elements.[6]

If an SS is finite, i.e., contains a finite number of expressions, then there must be an expression or expressions of maximal length. For example, if an SS is of order 6 and no expression is of length greater than 10, then, even if all combinations of length ≤ 10 are allowed, the maximum number of expressions is 6^{10}, which is

5. Some of the main expositions of set theory are: Erich Kamke, *Theory of Sets*, translated from the 2d German ed. (New York, 1950); Adolph Fraenkel, *Einleitung in die Mengenlehre* (Berlin, 1923); Felix Hausdorff, *Mengenlehre* (3d ed.; Berlin and Leipzig, 1935).

6. For Boolean algebras see the standard works on symbolic logic, particularly Paul C. Rosenbloom, *The Elements of Mathematical Logic* (New York, 1950).

finite. A language of infinite element order, however, must have an infinite number of expressions, even if there are expressions of maximum length. With regard to finiteness, then, there are four classes of systems: (1) those of finite order with expressions of a maximum length l; (2) those of finite order without maximum l; (3) those of infinite order with maximum l; and (4) those of infinite order without maximum l. Of these, members of the first class of systems have a finite number of expressions, the others an infinite number. In what follows, except where a statement is made to the contrary, we shall be concerned with systems of finite order and no maximum l. This is the class to which all natural languages belong.

Since any SS is contained in the homogeneous infinite SS of the same order (the system containing all permutations and combinations of the elements), the enunciation of grammatical rules is, in essence, the laying of bounds on this infinite system by setting limitations to the allowable permutations and combinations. A rule or set of rules is said to be "well determined" if it is sufficient to allow us to decide for any permutation and combination of its elements, i.e., for any member of the appropriate infinite system, whether the expression belongs to the system or not. The notion of "well-determination" is therefore a test of the adequacy of grammatical rules.

Rules are of a number of possible kinds. The following enumeration is not logically exhaustive.

I. *Cardinal rules.*—These rules have to do with the cardinal number of occurrences of a particular element in the expressions of an SS. They include the following: (1) rules of maxima and minima state that a given element may occur at the most n times or at the least n times in every expression; (2) rules of ratio specify that if two elements, x and y, appear in an expression, x/y is a constant; (3) rules of relative size state that if two elements, x and y, occur in an expression, the number of occurrences of y is $x + n$, where x is a constant.

Example: In an SS of order 5 with the elements specified as a, b, c, d, and e, if we have a rule that the maximum of c is 2, then, according to this well-determined rule, the expression *abcacd* is in the system, but *accdca* is not.

II. *Rules of transition.*—These are rules regarding the limitations on the occurrence of certain elements in certain positions if certain others are found in an expression. They are divided into positive and negative rules, depending on whether the element is required or excluded, and definite or indefinite, depending on whether the relative position of the required or excluded element is defined or not. An example of a positive definite transitional rule is the following: c must always be preceded by a with one other element intervening. An example of a negative indefinite rule is that d may not be preceded at any distance by b. In mathematics and written English, the requirement that an opening parenthesis must always be followed by a closing parenthesis at some interval is a rule of positive indefinite transition.

III. *Rules of infinite interpolation.*—First the elements are divided into two or more classes, which may, but need not, overlap. Every expression consists of some specified number of members of one or more, but not all, the classes and any number of occurrences (including zero) of members of the other classes. For example, we divide the elements *a, b, c, d, e*, into two classes, A, containing *a* and *b*, and B, containing *c, d,* and *e*. We then specify that every expression must contain one instance of a member of A and any number of instances of members of B. We might, as an additional rule, also require that the members of B always follow. On this basis, *bded, acc, b*, are in the system, but *de, cab, ba,* and *dca* are not. Rules of infinite interpolation are the model for linguistic rules of phrase expansion. They may be considered as rules of transition in which we operate not with individual elements but with classes of elements.

IV. *Rules of length.*—These rules exclude expressions of certain lengths, for example, all those expressions whose length is even. In fact, any monotonically increasing function whose domain is the entire set of positive integers and whose range is included in the positive integers will do, e.g., the function which assigns to each positive integral number *n* the *n*th prime number. In this case, all expressions whose length is a prime number are ungrammatical.

V. *Ordinal rules.*—We may make use of the functions just mentioned and apply them not to the length of the expressions but to an ordered set of all the expressions of Rule I. If we assign an order to each element, say, the alphabetic order, *a, b, c, d, e*, then we can first list expressions of length 1, then those of length 2, etc., and, within each, follow the dictionary rules of order: *a, b, c, d, e, aa, ab, ac, ad, ae, ba, bb, bc, bd, be, ca, cb, cc, cd, ce, da, db, dc, dd, de, ea, eb, ec, ed, ee, aaa, aab,* etc. Then all the values of some function as just described can be included in the system. If, in this case, the function is $y = 2x$ for positive integral x, then the second, fourth, sixth, etc., of the above expressions are grammatical, i.e., in the system, and the first, third, etc., are not.[7]

Instead of using elements as units in applying the foregoing rules, we can use specified finite sequences. For example, in an SS of element order 4 with the elements specified as *a, b, c, d*, we might form the following six sequences: *acdd, ba, ad, cc, a, bcdcd.* The number of such sequences is the sequence order of the SS, in this case six. I₆ with these specifications will consist of all possible permutations and combinations of these elements.[8] The same kinds of rules can be applied to sequences as to elements. For example, in the present case we can lay down a maximal rule that *ba* may not occur more than once in an expression and a length rule that all expressions contain an odd number of sequences. Then *acddcca* will be in the system, but *baadba* will not because, though of length 3, it contains *ba* twice. Likewise, *acddab* will not be in the system because it is not composed exclusively of the defined sequences. Systems without such sequences, like those of the earlier examples, may be considered limiting cases in which the element order and the sequence order are

7. Actually, all rules can be stated as ordinal rules if we apply the term "function" in a broad manner, as is usual in modern mathematics. The type described in the text under ordinal rules is a special case in which this method proves simplest. For further treatment of this topic see Appendix II, "On Ordinal Rules."

8. The convention is employed of uniting the element order at the upper right and the sequence order at the lower right.

the same and each sequence contains a single element. Since there will frequently be occasion to make statements referring equally to elements or sequences, it will be convenient to have a term "unit" to cover both cases. Similarly, in a system with sequences which are distinct from units, a given expression will contain an equal or greater number of sequences than of elements. To deal with this eventuality the terms "element length," "sequence length," and "unit length" will be employed in analogous fashion.

Various of the foregoing types of rules can be combined as simultaneous requirements. For example, we can require that c may not occur more than twice, that a never be immediately followed by b, and that all expressions have a length which is a multiple of 3. Then ccc will not be in the system, because, although its length is a multiple of 3, it contains more than 2 occurrences of c. Nor will $cabdec$ belong because, although its length is 6, a multiple of 3, and it does not contain more than 2 occurrences of c, it exhibits the forbidden sequence ab. It is clear that a system governed by a number of rules simultaneously contains only those expressions found in every one of the systems specified by each rule in isolation. It is therefore the intersection of these systems.

Such rules may apply to sign systems both with a finite and with an infinite number of expressions. Finite systems, however, need not conform to any of these rules but may consist of any arbitrary selection of the units. A listing of the allowed combinations is, in this case, a well-determined procedure, since any combination occurring in the list belongs to the system and any which is not found there is excluded. It is obvious that the procedure of listing is always open to us for finite systems but that rules, where possible, will be more convenient. There are also infinite systems defined as $I^n - F^n$, where F^n is some finite system of order n and I and F are homogeneous. Such systems may be defined by a negative list procedure if F^n cannot be defined except by list, for $I^n - F^n$ will consist of all those expressions not listed as belonging to F^n.

A semiotic must contain two distinct classes of procedures. By one, which may be called "synthetic," well-determined rules are stated, in accordance with which the expressions of a given SS may be constructed. The opposite procedure—analysis—which has not been considered in the discussion up to this point, is of particular interest to a science such as linguistics which operates with empirically given systems. The problem here is, given samples of expressions in the system, to derive an adequate set of rules. This involves many additional considerations. Initially, it may be pointed out, equal systems, that is, systems which contain exactly the same expressions, may be defined by different sets of rules. Such systems may be called "heteronomic." The following is a trivial example of heteronomy. The system of element order n (and sequence order n) with the length rule that all expressions must be of even length is equal to the system of element order n and sequence order n^2 without restriction on the combination of sequences. For $n = 3$ and specified elements a, b, c, with the former set of rules the expression $bcbacb$ is interpreted as of length 6 composed of the elements $a, b,$ and c, while with the latter it is interpreted as of length 3 and composed of the sequences *bc*, *ba*, and *cb*. We ask whether, among the various ways of formulating rules, there is one which is non-arbitrary. This is equivalent to asking for a procedure which, applied in every case, will pick out one solution among all the possible ones.

Analysis, moreover, raises the question of induction in acute form. Since our sample is always finite, if we have to do with an infinite system, we never know but that the next example will overthrow one of our rules. A form of quantitative inductive logic which assigns a degree of confirmation to each rule, such as that proposed by Carnap, may prove useful here.[9] To take a simple example, if a system has a rule that some element may not occur more than twice in any expression, this rule is better confirmed in one sample than in another if the sample contains a larger number of expressions, if the expressions are longer, and if the system has a smaller number of elements. In the latter instance the proportion of expressions which might break the rule is greater; hence the lack of negative instances in a given sample is a more powerful confirmation of the rule.

Two alternative methodologies are to be considered in testing rules. In the first of these we confine ourselves to a sample in which all the expressions have been spontaneously offered or elicited from the informant. We can then say, concerning any possible expression, whether it belongs to this corpus or not. If it does, it is an expression in the system. If it does not, we cannot reach a decision. We can merely wait to see whether it will occur or be elicited later. On this procedure we can sometimes say that an expression is in the system, but we can never definitively say that it is not.

The second method, which may be called that of the leading question, allows us greater latitude. On this procedure, we are permitted to make up any expression whatever and ask the informant whether it is in the system or not. As contrasted with the first method, it will sometimes allow us to say that an expression is not in the system. It provides a means of swift refutation of a rule in some instances, though not of confirmation. To illustrate, in the case of an element which may not occur more than twice, we make up an expression in which the element occurs three times, thus violating the rule. If the informant accepts the expression as in the system, the rule is decisively refuted.

Whether we allow ourselves the use of this second procedure is a purely empirical problem. If, for example, on one occasion an informant rejected an expression on the leading-question method and later used it spontaneously, we would doubt the validity of its use in this particular case. In what follows it will be assumed that a leading-question method can be legitimately employed.

In the remainder of this chapter, certain analytic notions of particular relevance to the grammatical analysis of natural languages will be developed. First to be considered are the related concepts of substitution and class. Given an expression of a particular SS and a specified unit within the expression, we can usually obtain another expression in the same system by replacing this unit with another of the same

---

9. See Rudolf Carnap, *Logical Foundations of Probability* (Chicago, 1950).

kind. The set of units resulting from such substitution, including the original unit itself, will be called a "contextual class." If the unit selected cannot be replaced by any other unit, then it is the only member of the contextual class. This can be illustrated by the following example. Let there be a total of ten permitted expressions of element length 3 in a given system, L_1, as follows:

1.	$a\ p\ x$		6.	$b\ q\ y$
2.	$a\ r\ x$		7.	$b\ r\ x$
3.	$a\ r\ y$		8.	$c\ p\ x$
4.	$b\ p\ y$		9.	$c\ p\ y$
5.	$b\ q\ x$		10.	$c\ s\ y$

If we consider x in the expression apx (1), we see that it cannot be replaced by any other element to obtain another expression of the system. Thus x by itself forms a contextual class with a single member. A class of two members arises if we hold a–x constant in the same expression apx (1), since r may replace p, producing arx (2). Therefore, this context class has p and r as its members. If, instead, we start from bpy (4) and hold b–y constant, we obtain a class containing p and q because of bqy (6), but excluding r. It is therefore seen that, in the same position, different classes arise, depending on the particular expression taken as the point of departure. A contextual class needs for its determination both the particular unit to be replaced by others and a context, namely, the expression in which it occurs. This is the reason for the choice of the term "contextual class." Other types of substitution leading to other kinds of classes will be considered later.

Another key concept is that of a "construction." If we describe a set of permitted expressions of the same unit length within an SS by specifying the class of units which may appear in each position, we are employing the basic notion of construction as used in grammar. Expressions belong to the same construction if they have members of the same classes in the same positions. Thus in English, with words as units, *John sees the house* and *William catches a ball* are members of the same construction. Since we are often concerned with relations among expressions of different unit length which are related in certain specified ways to be considered later and which have a similar internal structure, it will be expedient to extend the term "construction" to such cases. Thus *John sees the house* and *John sees the large house* will be members of the same construction although of unit length 4 and 5, respectively, while *Mary's dress was green*, although of unit length 4, belongs to a different construction. The term "subconstruction" will be reserved for expressions of the same unit length which belong to the same construction. Systems which, like natural languages, have no expression of maximal length cannot be described in terms of subconstructions alone, since we would have to define the subconstructions of each length, leading to an infinity of definitions.

The set of expressions of a given unit length of a particular SS can always be described in terms of subconstructions, though this will not always be the most expedient procedure. It should also be noted at this point that the description by subconstructions is relative to the procedure used to determine classes, the method of contextual classes already described being but one of a number of alternatives. The following distinctions which are applicable to subconstructions of any kind will be employed. If the class in each position of the subconstruction has the same membership, the subconstruction will be termed "homogeneous," otherwise "heterogeneous." Linguistic subconstructions are always heterogeneous. Subconstructions in which all possible sequences involving members of the successive classes are expressions of the system will be called "perfect," otherwise "imperfect." Thus, if a subconstruction of element length 2 is described as consisting of the class $\{a, b\}$ followed by the class $\{c, d\}$ and if ac, bd, ad, and bd all occur, the subconstruction is perfect; if any one of these is not an expression, then it is imperfect. Description in terms of imperfect subconstructions is not very useful because all non-occurring sequences must somehow be specified in addition to the rule of the subconstruction. Finally, it is important to distinguish those analyses in which two expressions of the same length cannot belong to two different subconstructions, that is, in which all the subconstructions are mutually exclusive from those in which this condition does not hold. Those in which the subconstructions are mutually exclusive will be called "unambiguous"; those for which this is not true, "ambiguous."

The subconstructions arrived at by the use of contextual classes as defined above are, in general, imperfect and ambiguous. If, for example, in L_1 we start with apx (1) we generate the initial contextual class $\{a, c\}$ because of cpx (8). In the second position, the class is $\{p, r\}$ because of arx (2). In the final position we have the class consisting of x only. The subconstruction consists, then, of the classes $\{a, c\}$, $\{p, r\}$, and $\{x\}$ in that order. It is an imperfect subconstruction because crx does not occur, and it is ambiguous because if, for example, we started with arx (2) as our initial expression, we would derive a subconstruction consisting of the succession $\{a, b\}$, $\{r\}$, and $\{x, y\}$ and the expression arx (2) belongs to both this subconstruction and the one described above which employed apx (1) as its starting point.

Methods of defining other than contextual classes will now be considered. An operation to be called "horizontal transformation" is introduced at this point. Any expression Y will be said to be derived from another expression X by a horizontal transformation, in symbols, $X \rightarrow Y$, if Y results from X by replacing a single unit in X by another one of the same kind. Thus, in L_1, bqx (5) $\rightarrow bqy$ (6). This relation is, of course, symmetrical: if $X \rightarrow Y$, then always $Y \rightarrow X$. If we apply a succession of transformations, beginning, as before when contextual classes were formed, with apx (1) of L_1, we generate arx (2) by apx (1) $\rightarrow arx$ (2) as before, giving us p and r in the second position, but the chains apx (1) $\rightarrow cpx$ (8) $\rightarrow cpy$ (9) $\rightarrow csy$ (10) produce q and s also in the second position, so that the entire class consists of $\{p, q, r, s\}$. The same class will eventuate by the method of horizontal transformation, regardless of which expression in L_1 is taken as the starting point. Such a class will be called an "extended class." Similarly, the extended class of the first position will have the membership $\{a, b, c\}$ and that of the third position $\{x, y\}$. All the expressions of L_1 will belong to the subconstruction consisting of the succession of these three classes $\{a, b, c\}$, $\{p, q, r, s\}$, and $\{x, y\}$. That is, by horizontal transformation all the expressions of L_1 can be reached from any one as a starting point, so that they are members of the same subconstruction. However, this subconstruction will be imperfect, since many expressions formed from the succession of classes which defines it do not belong to L_1, for example, *bry*. A subconstruction defined in this manner by a succession of extended classes will be called an "extended subconstruction."

It is not, in general, true, as happens in this case, that all expressions of a given unit length are members of the same extended subconstruction. We might construct, for example, a system L_2 of element order 4, without sequences and with its elements specified as *a*, *b*, *c*, and *d*. Let there be the following rule of indefinite negative transition: If an expression contains *a*, it does not contain *c*; if it contains *a*, it does not contain *d*; if it contains *b*, it does not contain *c*; and if it contains *b*, it does not contain *d*. In other words, every expression is composed either of *a*'s or *b*'s exclusively or of *c*'s or *d*'s exclusively. For any expression of any given element length, we cannot reach by horizontal transformation any expression containing *c* or *d* from one containing *a* or *b*, or vice versa. Thus the expressions of any given length fall into two extended subconstructions which are mutually exclusive. In general, horizontal transformation will produce extended constructions which are mutually exclusive, that is, unambiguous, because the relation of being connected by a chain of such transformations is an equality, that is, it is reflexive, symmetrical, and transitive.

We have seen that the extended class gives us unambiguous but imperfect constructions. The question arises whether it is possible to describe a procedure for defining class which will create subconstructions that are at once unambiguous and perfect. This can be accomplished, but, in contrast to the extended class, it involves a restriction rather than an expansion of the contextual class and, with it, an increase, in general, in the number of subconstructions. The importance of operations based on the restricted class will become evident when the problem of defining the word is discussed in the following chapter.

"Restricted class" is defined in the following manner. We allow substitution of one unit for another in an expression only if, for all expressions of the system obtained from the original expression by the addition or removal of units, there exist corresponding expressions in which the substituted expression occurs and, vice versa, if there is any expression obtained from the substituted expression by addition or removal of units, the corresponding expression with the original unit also belongs to the system. If, for example, *apy* is an expression and *aqy* is likewise an expression, *q* may be substituted for *p* and is a member of the same contextual class. For *p* and *q* to be members of the same restricted class, it will be demanded in addition that if, for example, *apny* exists, *aqny* must also be an expression of the language; and if *aqyr* exists, that *apyr* should exist also. If this condition fails in any case, then *p* and *q* do not belong to the same restricted class.

On the whole, the restricted class is the most useful in grammatical, particularly syntactic, analysis. In English, for example, with words as units, we can substitute *well* for *houses* in *I see houses* to obtain *I see well*. It would obviously be unsatisfactory to consider *houses* and *well* as members of the same class, since we would like to assert that these two sentences belong to differing constructions and that *houses* and *well* belong to different classes, the former being a noun and the latter an adverb. Applying the notion of restricted class, *houses* and *well* will belong to different classes, and consequently the two sentences will belong to different subconstructions. We can, for example, expand *I see well* to *I see very well*, but the corresponding expression *I see very houses* does not occur. Hence *well* and *houses* belong to the same contextual, but different restricted, classes. It is usually said that *houses* and *well* belong to the same class but that classes of this kind are not useful in grammatical description. The employment of restricted classes enables us to distinguish those instances of substitution in which we substitute one member of the same restricted class for another, as in the substitution of *rooms* for *houses* in *I see houses*, and those in which we substitute one restricted class for another restricted class, as in the substitution of *well* for *houses* in the same sentence. Disregarding minor complications, it is possible to distinguish inflectional from root elements in this manner by a purely formal procedure. An inflectional morpheme cannot be replaced by another morpheme without changing the restricted subconstruction, while the root can be replaced by another root without changing it.

One further method of defining classes should be mentioned which diverges radically from those previously discussed, in that it does not involve substitution of a particular unit within an expression but rather involves the abstracting of certain partially similar forms from their context. Thus in Latin we say that every noun consists of a stem followed by an inflection, and we set up classes of inflections for each model of nominal declension, such as {us, ī, ō, um, ō; ī, ōrum, īs, ōs, īs} for the second declension. As has just been seen, inflectional morphemes are distinguished precisely by the fact that they cannot be substituted for one another without changing the restricted construction. In comparing the same stem with different inflections, we are thus abstracting them from their contexts. In the following chapter in the discussion of the morpheme, the initial and final members of an inflectional field, as there defined, are formed in abstraction from context. Such classes will be called "non-contextual." We might consider that the analyst is setting up a new finite language whose sequences are certain members of the full language he is analyzing and that within this finite language he employs once again the technique of horizontal transformation.[10]

Thus far, only those internal transformations have been considered by which we move among expressions of the same unit length within the same subconstruction.

---

10. In addition to restricted and extended classes, others are possible. If we are allowed to substitute in any preceding position but not in any following, then we have the "regressive class." If we can move through substitution transformations only in the positions following but not in preceding, we have the "progressive class." Still narrower classes are generated by restricting substitution to the immediately following, that following at an interval of one, etc. In the example discussed in the text, the progressive class of p in cpx is $\{p, s\}$ generated by the transformations $cpx \rightarrow cpy \rightarrow csy$.

For example, in L_2 above, there are two subconstructions of element length 3, one containing expressions exclusively made up of the elements a and b, the other of expressions composed only of c and d. Likewise, for length 4, there will be two subconstructions. It is obvious that there is a certain relationship between the subconstruction of length 3 containing only a and b and that of length 4 containing only a and b which does not hold between that of length 3 containing a and b and that of length 4 containing c and d and so with the two subconstructions containing only c and d. Those which are so connected can be reached from each other by a vertical transformation. Such a transformation is no longer one to one, since the number of expressions is greater in the subconstruction of greater length. We can, however, set up a definite rule which will produce the entire set of combinations of length $n + 1$ from that of n and then that of $n + 2$ from that of $n + 1$, etc. Thus in L_2 all the expressions belonging to the subconstruction containing c and d of length 4 are generated by a one-to-two vertical transformation of each member of the corresponding subconstruction of length 3 ($bdd \rightarrow bddb$; $bbd \rightarrow bbdd$; $ddb \rightarrow ddbb$; $ddb \rightarrow ddbd$, etc.).

All the subconstructions of various length which can be reached from the subconstruction of shortest length (called the "basis") form a construction.

Sometimes what is a single subconstruction on the basis of the rule of horizontal transformation must be divided into several parts, each of which is a member of a different construction. The expressions through which one moves from one such subconstruction to another are ambiguous expressions which belong to two constructions. However, on expansion through vertical transformation, the two parts expand differently and are therefore members of two different constructions. In the written English of newspaper headlines, therefore, without intonations "bears fly" is an ambiguous expression, through which, by horizontal transformations, members of two different constructions can be reached from each other: *birds fly → bears fly → bears twins*. However, *birds fly* expands, for example, to *large birds fly*, whereas *large bears twins* is not an expansion; and *bears twins* expands to *bears healthy twins*, whereas *birds healthy fly* is not an expansion.

Every expression belongs to some construction, and no expression except the ambiguities just described belongs simultaneously to two constructions. An SS can therefore be divided completely into constructions. Such a division is a constructional partition of the system.[11] An SS is composed of the union of all its constructions, each of which is therefore a subsystem. Each such subsystem, which may be considered a system in its own right, contained in the larger system is, in turn, the intersection of one or more subsystems, each specified by a rule, as was noted earlier. The logical form of an SS is therefore the union of constructions, each of which is the intersection of subsystems, each defined by a single rule. As limiting cases, a system may consist of a single construction, or a construction may be defined by a single

11. There are other means than constructions for partitioning the expressions of a system. For example, we can have a length partition, in which each expression of odd length is put in one subsystem and each of even length in the other.

rule. In symbols, the logical form of an SS is: $(a_1 \cap a_2 \cap a_3 \ldots) \cup (b_1 \cap b_2 \cap b_3 \ldots) \cup (c_1 \cap c_2 \cap c_3 \ldots) \cup \ldots$, which reduces in the limiting case of the infinite language of some order to a_1.

The subconstruction of shortest length of a construction will be called the "basis," the other subconstructions the "expansion." The rules for a construction can most easily be stated by a device analogous to that employed for infinite sequences in mathematics. The first few subconstructions are written in order of length. The symbols indicate an extended class of elements in sequences, whichever the unit. A construction in which each length has a single subconstruction is called "linear," while one in which each length has a larger number of subconstructions than the previous one is called "ramified." Those of different length are here separated by a vertical line. The following are examples of constructions written in the manner described:

I. A|AB|ABB|ABBB| ...
II. A|BA, AB|ABB, BAB, BBA| ...
III. AB|CAB, ACB, ABC|CCAB, CACB, CABC, ACCB, ACBC, ABCC| ...

Here, I is linear; II and III are ramified. A class which appears in every subconstruction is basic, one which appears only in the expansion is non-basic. If a class x never appears in a subconstruction without another class y, while y occurs in some subconstruction without x, then x modifies y.

In I above, A is basic, B non-basic, and B modifies A. We may have a construction in which A modifies B and B modifies C, as with noun, adjective, and adverb in English. These are the "ranks" of Jespersen.

In any construction at any point there is a possibility of infinite insertion. For example, in CAB, the second item of III, an indefinite number of C's can be inserted between C and A or between A and B (cf. the rules of infinite interpolation mentioned in the earlier part of this chapter). If two classes were not to allow of interpolation between them, i.e., appear in immediate succession in all subconstructions in which they occur, they would be considered a single extended class. The property of infinite interpolation at boundaries will figure as an essential part of the definition of the word in the next essay, and it will be shown that the word in language is the unit of linguistic constructions.

In general, no unit corresponding to the morpheme can be discovered in uninterpreted systems, i.e., without knowledge of meanings. It is a corollary of the present analysis that the word boundaries of natural language can be located without recourse to meaning but that morphemic boundaries, in general, cannot. It might be thought that all that is necessary to isolate morphemes would be to decompose the sequences into smaller recurring subsequences. An example will show that, without the test of meaning, this will not isolate units equivalent to the morpheme. If, in English, in a single extended class we find *trip*, *sip*, *trail*, and *sail*, only a knowledge of the meanings will prevent us from making the recurrent partials *tr-*, *s-*, *-ip*, and

-*ail* subsequences. Certain kinds of subsequences, however, can be discovered in uninterpreted systems. The problem is of interest in showing the limits of analysis without meaning. This is possible only if the formation is entirely regular, that is, if two extended classes are isomorphic, so that they can be put into one-to-one correlation. Thus each member of one of the classes B might, by the constant addition of some element or elements, produce the corresponding member of the other class.[12] If there are irregularities, we shall not always know which member of B correlates with some given member of B'. In the English verb, without meaning, we shall not know whether *say* or *see* is the present of *saw*. Calling two such isomorphic classes B and B', the three possible cases are exemplified by the following sets of constructions:

CASE 1. INFLECTION

I. A, AB, ABB . . .
II. C, CB', CB'B' . . .

Here the difference between B and B' allows them to function in different constructions, e.g., singular and plural. The elements constant for each correlated pair of B and B' will be the stem, and the parts which are different, the inflection. If, in Turkish, B contains *evi* "the house" (acc.) and in B' the correlated member is *evde* "in the house," *ev-* is the stem and *-i* and *-de* are inflections:

CASE 2. AGREEMENT

I. BC,|BCC, BCD|,|BCCC, BCCD, BCDD| . . .
II. B'C',|B'C'C', B'C'D|,|B'C'C'C', B'C'C'D, B'C'DD| . . .

This is similar to case 1, except that two classes are involved which show corresponding differences in different constructions. In English, B would be the class of singular nouns and C the class of verbs in agreement with them, B' the class of plural nouns and C' the class of verbs in agreement:

CASE 3. EXOCENTRIC DERIVATION

I. A, AB, ABB . . .
II. C, CD, CDD . . .
(D = B' + K)

Here members of B' correlated to those of B function in a different construction, but, in addition, non-correlated members K form another subclass of the same class D. Hence the transformation into B' has shifted the members of B into another class, functioning in a different construction. In English *-er*, which makes a noun when added to any verb, illustrates this case. The class of verbs will correspond to members of B of the example, agent nouns such as *sing-er* to members of B', non-agent nouns to K, and the total class of nouns to D. Hence *-er* will be a derivational element and *sing-* a stem:

12. This situation can also be dealt with through other concepts of set theory not yet mentioned. See Appendix III on "The External Transformation of Sign Systems."

CASE 4. ENDOCENTRIC DERIVATION

I. A, AD, ADD . . .

(D = B + B′)

Here the members of D fall into two groups, B and B′, in one-to-one correlation, and all function in the same construction. There is no logical reason for excluding the case of more than two subgroups, say, B, B′, B″ and B‴, all in one-to-one correspondence with one another. This is perfectly regular derivation in which all the members of the class participate. This case is rare in actual languages. A perfectly regular set of personal possessive affixes to a noun class with which all nouns occurred would be an example.

It is possible to show, in terms of the concepts just discussed, that, in general, where the rules of an infinite system have been formulated by reference to two levels—an element level and a sequence level—the process of analysis will also lead inevitably to the same distinction. This can be most easily understood by reference to an example. We set up an infinite system L_3 of element order 6, the elements being specified as a, b, c, d, e, f, and of sequence order 10 with sequences ab, bc, bd, db, df, fe, abd, abe, dec. There are to be no limitations to the combinations of these sequences. If we take the elements as our point of departure, it is clear that there will be no expressions of element length 1; 6 of element length 2 (ab, bc, bd, db, df); 4 of element length 3 (abd, abe, cbd, dec); and 36 of element length 4 ($abab$, $abbc$, $abbd$, $abdb$, $abdf$, $abfc$, $bcab$, $bcbc$, $bcbd$, $bcdb$, $bcdf$, $bcfc$, $bdab$, $bdbc$, $bdbd$, $bddb$, $bddf$, $bdfc$, etc.). Using elements as our units of substitution, the 6 expressions of length 2 will fall into three subconstructions [(1) ab, (2) $fc → bc → bd$, (3) $db → df$]. The expressions of length 3 will divide into three subconstructions [(1) $abd → abe$, (2) acd, (3) cbd]. The 36 expressions of length 4 will be analyzable into nine subconstructions. There will be no rule of vertical transformation which will carry us from the subconstructions of length 2 to those of length 3 or from length 3 to length 4. It is true that we can expand from length 2 to length 4, which is not in accord with our rule for forming constructions out of subconstructions, by moving always from length n to length $n + 1$. Even this, however, can be done only by treating various sequences of two elements as units. Thus we can move from the subconstruction of length 2, which contains $db → df$, to that of length 4, which contains $dbfc → dbbc → dbbd$, $dfbd → dfbc → dffc$, but only by adding fc, bc, and bd as units. It is thus impossible to form a construction which accords with the rules described by employing the elements as units. Once we treat the ten sequences enumerated above as units, we attain the following results. Expressions of every sequence length occur, including 1. For every length there is only one subconstruction, and the subconstructions of any length $n + 1$ are derivable by a simple vertical transformation from that of length n. In this case, two levels are necessary, and analysis forces us to employ what synthesis has postulated.

Infinite systems are of two kinds: those with sequence level distinct from element level and those in which the two coincide. Language is of the former type, the elements being the phonemes, and the sequences the words. In such systems there are two fundamental branches of grammar: the study of the composition of sequences out of elements and the study of the functions of sequences in constructions. These infra-sequential and supra-sequential aspects are morphology and syntax, respectively, in the case of language. An indefinite number of infra-sequential levels can be set up. Thus there will be an additional level between the element and sequence level if all sequences are composed of certain arbitrary subsequences not all of which are single elements. So on the supra-sequential level there may be units, such as the phrases and clauses of language, which can be conveniently described in terms of parts which are themselves constructions involving sequences. But in every system there must be elements and hence an element level, and if there are no expressions of maximal length, as is always true in natural languages, there must be infinite vertical transformations defining each of a finite number of constructions; else there will be an infinite number of rules, and the SS will not be well determined. Units of this transformation must exist. There are then two cases, either the units of this expansion are the same as the elements, in which case the levels fall together, or they are distinct. Mathematics is a single-level system, where each symbol corresponds both to the phoneme and to the word, while natural languages are two-level systems.

CHAPTER II

THE DEFINITION OF LINGUISTIC UNITS

THE MORPHEME

THE morpheme has figured in American linguistics, along with the phoneme, as a basic unit of analysis.[1] It is perhaps most commonly characterized as the minimal sequence of phonemes which has a meaning or, negatively, as the smallest succession of phonemes which bears no phonetic-semantic resemblance to any other sequence. While these statements can be considered useful adumbrations of the general nature of the morphemic unit, it is generally realized that further, more precise rules are needed for an operational definition which can actually be applied. There is, by now, a fairly considerable literature on the morpheme, and the differences among the procedures advocated by different writers have led some to doubt its usefulness altogether. From the present exposition it will be clear that a number of independent procedures are involved in defining the morpheme and that, for several of these, plausible and equally valid choices are open. In other words, the assumptions of morphemic analysis are rather complex, and a fairly large number of alternative definitions are possible. It may be said in justification of the morpheme that it has in many instances proved a useful unit in descriptions. It has most frequently perhaps been utilized in grammatical analyses of American Indian languages. The present exposition will seek to explicate existing practice in this matter, that is, to show what logical assumptions are being made and to state them, if possible, in rigorous form.

In addition to the requirement that the unit be minimal, that is, that it should not contain smaller units of the same kind, and that it have a meaning, others are usually sought. We expect that every expression of a language should be segmentable into an integral number of morphemes in such a way that every phoneme belongs to some morpheme and that no phoneme belongs to more than one. This will be called the requirement of "morphemic accountability."[2] We also require that every word boundary be a morpheme boundary, while the reverse need not be true. That is, every word should consist of a finite integral number of morphemes, but as a special case the number of morphemes may be one. The definition of an isolating language

---

1. Note that in European linguistics *morpheme* often designates an inflectional element, as opposed to *semanteme*, a root or stem.

2. The term and the concept originate with Charles F. Hockett, "Problems of Morphemic Analysis," *Language*, XXIII (1947), 321–43. However, it will appear later that in some instances a phoneme cannot be assigned without arbitrariness to one of two morphemes and is thus considered part of both.

is presumably one in which the morpheme coincides with the word, that is, no word may be divided into smaller units which have a meaning.

A distinction is usually made between the morph and the morpheme, somewhat analogous to that between the phone (phonetic variant) and the phoneme. If we segment expressions into minimal meaningful parts, we arrive at units called "morphs." It would seem natural, in seeking to describe the language as a whole, to count every morph as different which differs either in the phonemes it contains or in its meaning. But in practice this does not turn out to be a very useful way of proceeding, since it ignores many resemblances among morphs which are relevant to a grammatical description. For example, in English, we might segment the following two expressions into morphs: I. (1) *a* (2) *leaf* (3) *fall-* (4) *-s* (5) *from* (6) *the* (7) *tree*; II. (1) *two* (2) *leav-* (3) *-es* (4) *fall* (5) *from* (6) *the* (7) *tree*. Applying the proposed rule that two morphs be considered distinct if they differ either phonemically or semantically, *leaf* in I and *leav-* in II would be considered separate units, as different as, say, *leaf* and *fall*. Moreover, in exactly the same two constructions, a single unchanging morph, such as *twig*, may occur in place of both *leaf* and *leav-*. This situation is met by setting up a larger unit, a morpheme, containing the morphs *leaf* and *leav-* as members. Such members of the same morpheme are termed "allomorphs," and the alternation in form among allomorphs is called "morphophonemic alternation."

In the light of this distinction between morphs and morphemes and of the general aims of morphemic analysis as described here, there are three fundamental problems: (1) In a given expression, how many morphs are there? This may be called the "problem of morph determination." (2) How can every phoneme be assigned to some morph unambiguously? This is the "problem of morph boundaries." (3) Which morphs shall be assigned to the same morphemes? This is the "problem of morpheme determination."

We turn, first, to the problem of determining the number of morphs in a given expression. There are clearly divisions which are justified and which every analyst would make. For example, everyone would divide English *eating* into two morphs, *eat-* and *-ing*. There are just as obviously other divisions which are arbitrary. Thus the analysis of *chair* into *ch-*, "wooden object," and *-air*, "something to sit on," would be universally rejected. Yet, given the vagueness of the term "similarity" when unaccompanied by any operational specifications, why should we not, in accordance with the statement that a morph should not show partial phonetic-semantic resemblance to some other form, note the similarity of *chair* to *chest*, also an object made of wood, and so justify the previous analysis and add *-est*, "object for storing," to our collection of morphs? It is true that such divisions are repudiated by everyone, but their repudiation should follow from our definitions. Alongside the generally accepted and the generally rejected divisions just cited, there is a considerable intermediate area of uncertainty in which opinions differ and with which we must be able to deal. Should, for example, English *deceive* be analyzed into *de-* and *-ceive?*

To provide an assured base, we start with a set of forms henceforth to be called a "square." A square exists when there are four expressions in a language which take the form AC, BC, AD, BD. An example is English *eating*:*walking*::*eats*:*walks*, where A is *eat-*, B is *walk-*, C is *-ing*, and D is *-s*. One of the four members may be zero, as in *king*:*kingdom*::*duke*:*dukedom*, where C is zero. Where a square exists with corresponding variation in meaning, we are justified in segmenting each of the four member sequences. Once it has been segmented, in a manner to be described later, each subsequence may again be tested for membership in a square. A test of correspondence of meaning is applied to avoid such squares as *hammer*:*ham*::*badger*:*badge*. We can formalize the semantic test by a somewhat pedantic translation procedure. If some other language can be found into which the translation of our four items likewise provides a square, we have a result which can hardly be accidental and may be considered evidence for the semantic correspondences. For example, the translation of the first square cited into Italian produces *mangiando*:*passeggiando*::*mangia*:*passeggia*.

A square conforming to these conditions will always give valid and generally accepted analyses. The method is too severe, however, in that it excludes some segmentations which everyone would want to allow. The first extension which we make is the following: A sequence which occurs with a member of a square is also recognized in sequences which do not form a square, provided (*a*) that the sequence of phonemes is identical except for phonologic changes (for which see below) and (*b*) that the meaning is the same. The remainder also becomes a morph on the basis of the principle of accountability. Thus we segment *huckleberry*, although it does not figure in any square, since a part of it, *berry*, is a morph elsewhere. This leaves the remainder *huckle-* also as a morph, although it never occurs in a square. If now *huckle-* were to occur in some other combination, we would recognize a segmentation there also and so add a new morph. This process is continued until we reach a sequence that does not recur in any other combination. In this instance we have reached it with *huckle-*. This whole procedure may be called "extension."

The problem of sameness of meaning in doubtful cases may also be met here by a translation test. In this case, can we find a language in which the term translated into English as *huckleberry* contains a portion which can be translated into English as *berry*? A German dictionary gives *amerikanische Heidelbeere*, which contains *Beere*, the German term which translates "berry" in the same dictionary.[3]

3. Instead of resorting to translation, one could, of course, say that the fact that a huckleberry is a berry is guaranteed by the respectable science of botany. What, then, of such cases as German *Walfisch*, "whale"? One might inquire whether *Fisch* when alone corresponds in use to the scientific definition of "fish." The definition "animal that lives in the sea" is as consistent and usable as the scientific one. But suppose, as is sometimes the case, that *Fisch* has the same meaning in popular and scientific discourse, in other words, that we have a historical survival? If so, we might justify it by a current belief in the great similarity of whales to fishes, but there remains the problem of measuring similarity. Note that an appeal to the speakers as to whether they think a whale is a fish or a whale is very much like a fish is different from asking them if *Walfisch* contains "whale" as a part, which is evidence regarding folk linguistics but not regarding the scientific analysis of the form.

Further morph segmentations, which are usual in practice, can be subsumed under what may be called a "formally defective square." We should like to analyze *men* into two morphs, one with the meaning "man" and the other with the meaning "plural," but there is no square into which it can be put. Such approximations as *man:men::boy:boys* are formally defective, in that they do not fall into segments of the pattern AC:BC::AD:BD. A segmentation into morphs is accepted if, first, a square can be found, like the formally defective one just quoted, in which the meaning differences correspond and in which the second pair itself figures in a perfect square (e.g., *boy:boys::lad:lads*). It is further required that all the prior members of each pair have some environment in which only they may occur, while there is at least one other distinct environment in which only the latter members of each pair can be found and that the prior members of all the pairs can be brought into approximate one-to-one relation to the latter members of each pair on the basis of meaning. In carrying out this environment complementation and one-to-one matching, all other formally imperfect pairs are considered, e.g., *tooth:teeth* as well as *man:men*.

This may be illustrated as follows: There is an environment in which prior members of the pairs which make up the squares can be placed and no other: *This* —— *is good* (man, boy, lad, tooth, etc.). There is another environment in which only the latter member of each pair may occur: *These* —— *are good*. Moreover, practically all members of one can be put into one-to-one correlation with the other: *man* → *men; boy* → *boys; house* → *houses; book* → *books; tooth* → *teeth;* etc. There are rare exceptions, like "people," which belongs to the latter class without a corresponding member of the former class.

This rather complicated statement is meant to restrict formally defective squares to members differing by the presence of different inflections, e.g., singular and plural in the examples given. This may seem a rather odd requirement, but it accords with general practice in morphemic analysis, and good reasons can be advanced in favor of it.

If we did not restrict the formally imperfect square to inflections, we might analyze *cow* into two morphs on the example of the formally imperfect square *bull:cow::lion:lioness*. For note that, in allowing the formally imperfect square, we have abandoned the criterion of phonetic similarity. However stated, the difference between *man* and *men* has no phonetic resemblance to the /-z/ of *boys*. If we permitted the formally imperfect square in non-inflectional squares, many analyses, considered generally unacceptable, would result, and it would be hard to know where to draw the line. Moreover, it is generally believed that segmentation is required in such cases as *men* for grammatical purposes. That is, in our grammar we take note of the difference between *man* and *men* in terms of a category of singular and plural, whereas the difference between *cow* and *bull* is purely lexical and only noted, by implication, in our dictionary. Such analyses are not to be confused with segmentations into two or more semantic categories where no perfect square exists as a model. In Latin, for example, we cannot analyze *-us*, "nominative singular," into two morphemes, nominative and singular. The square *-us*:*-ŏ*::*-ĭ*:*-īs*—"nominative singular":"dative singular"::"nominative plural":"dative plural"—does not contain a pair which can be substituted for members of a formally perfect square; hence this rule does not permit the segmentation of *-us*.

Corresponding to formally defective squares, we have those which are semantically defective. Here, if there are formally perfect non-phonologic variations, the analysis is permitted, even though definite meanings cannot be assigned to the morphs. Thus the sets *deceive*:*receive*::*decep-tion*:*recep-tion*::*decei-t*:*recei(p)-t* justify the divisions *de* + *ceive* and *re* + *ceive*. Without this rule, the usual assumption of morphs for the derived forms of verbs in Semitic languages would be impossible in the absence of consistent meaning correspondences to the extensive sets of phonetically parallel forms. The attempt to describe these Semitic forms without such segmentations would reduce Semitic grammar to virtual chaos.

It is worth noting that, just as in the formally imperfect square the criterion of phonetic similarity has been abandoned, so the criterion of resemblance of meaning is dispensed with in the semantically imperfect square. In both cases the justification is essentially the same: their convenience—indeed, their practical indispensability—for a coherent grammatical description of a language if we are to use the morpheme. On the other hand, both rules, as enunciated previously, put sharp limitations on the employment of these procedures, so that we are not led into segmentations which would generally be regarded as arbitrary and unjustifiable.

One more decision must be made before the rules of morph determination are complete. In perfect squares, if one of the segments is zero, for example, in English *nose*:*noses*::*rose*:*roses*, we must decide whether the forms containing this zero are made up of one morph or two, i.e., if *nose* and *rose* are one morph or two. Either procedure has advantages and disadvantages. In order to provide a complete definition of the morpheme, a decision is made here in favor of segmentation only where the difference is an inflectional one, for reasons similar to those discussed earlier in connection with the formally imperfect square.

From this exposition it can be seen that there are five distinct criteria for accepting a form as morphemically complex: (1) occurrence in a perfect square, (2) extension from a perfect square, (3) occurrence in a formally imperfect square, (4) occurrence in a semantically imperfect square, and (5) occurrence as a zero in a perfect square. Any of these can be accepted while others are rejected, except that it does not seem possible to reject No. 1 and accept any of the others. Moreover, No. 1 would probably meet with universal approval. A considerable variety of definitions of the morph is thus possible.

The next problem to be considered is that of morph boundaries. It might be thought that for formally perfect squares all that is needed is to assign the phonemes of each of our segments A, B, C, and D to its corresponding morph. Such a segmentation is given by the very fact of the existence of a formally perfect square, and it produces satisfactory results in the examples cited. Thus in *eating*:*walking*::*eats*:*walks*, the segments A *eat-*, B *walk-*, C *-ing*, and D *-s* give divisions *eat-ing*, *walk-ing*, *eat-s*, *walk-s*, which everyone would presumably find acceptable. However, such an example as *walking*:*talking*::*walks*:*talks*, where A is *w-*, B is *t-*, C is *-alking* /-ohkiŋ/, and D is *-alks* /-ohks/ shows that the matter is not so simple. Not just any square will do, and different squares produce different divisions of the same form. Moreover, although this was not stated explicitly before, there is no need for segments A, B, C, and D to be continuous. We require only the same order of phonemes and, where interrupted, the same length of interval belonging to another segment. This can be illustrated from classical Arabic *qatala*, "he killed":*ḍaraba*, "he struck":: *qutilu·*, "they were killed":*ḍuribu·*, "they were struck," where A is *q-t-l-*, B is *ḍ-r-b-*, C is *-a-a-a*, and D is *-u-i-u·*. Applying this consistently to English, the square *beats*:*breaks*::*beating*:*breaking* will divide *beats* into *b-s* and *-eat-*.

TABLE 1

	A	B	C	D	E
1.............	sleeps	sleep	sleeping	slept	slept
2.............	weeps	weep	weeping	wept	wept
3.............	keeps	keep	keeping	kept	kept
4.............	puts	put	putting	put	put
5.............	hits	hit	hitting	hit	hit
6.............	shakes	shake	shaking	shook	shaken
7.............	takes	take	taking	took	taken
					etc.

It will prove convenient at this point to make use of a terminology introduced by Wells.[4] The common part of two forms will be their "communis," the remainder of each one its "propria." Thus the communis of *eats* and *eating* will be *eat-*, the propria of *eats* will be *-s* and of *eating*, *-ing*.

The root of the difficulty described here is that the same form may figure in a number of different perfect squares. We therefore set forth in an array all the perfect squares in which a particular form figures. Establishing the convention that forms whose communis precedes their propria are written in a row and those whose propria precedes their communis are written in a column, it is possible to write them in such a manner that any four forms, two of which are in the same column and two of which are in the same row, form a perfect square. Such an array will be called a "restricted array." We construct an extended array from a restricted array by adding those forms which enter perfect squares with the forms of the restricted array even when they are not in a perfect square with the forms with which we started. Table 1 contains part of the restricted and extended array of *sleeps*.

The forms set off in the lower right-hand corner belong to the extended, but not the restricted, array of *sleeps*. The remainder belong to both.

By the "total communis" is meant the common part of all the forms in some row or column. Thus the total communis of A is /s/, of 5 is /hit/, and of 7 is /t-k/. Sometimes a total communis does not exist; in this case the forms fall into mutually ex-

4. Rulon S. Wells, "Automatic Alternation," *Language*, XXV (1949), 99–116.

clusive classes, each of which has a communis, called the "partial communis." Thus Column D in Table 1 has no total communis, but there are two partials, /t/ and /uk/, -ook-. We are now ready to state a set of rules for the assignment of phonemes to morphs in perfect squares.

1. Any phoneme which is a member of the total communis of a row belongs to the initial morph of the forms on the row; any phoneme which is a member of the total communis of a column belongs to the final morph of the forms in the column.

2. Any phoneme which belongs to the partial communis of its row and neither to the total nor to the partial communis of its column belongs to the initial morph, and, correspondingly, any phoneme which belongs to the partial communis of its column and neither to the total nor to the partial communis of its row belongs to the final morph.

3. Any phoneme which belongs to the partial communis of both its row and its column is inherently doubtful. It may be called a "merger phoneme."

4. Any phoneme which does not belong to a communis of either its row or its column is also inherently doubtful. If, however, it is both preceded and followed by phonemes already assigned to the same morph, it may be assigned to it also, to avoid discontinuities.

The following are applications of these rules to Table 1. In the form *sleeps* /slijps/, *s*, *l*, and *p* are definitely assigned to the initial morph by Rule 1, since its members belong to the total communis of Column A, and *s* to the final morph by the same rule. The remainder *ij* falls under Rule 4 and is assigned to the initial morph because it is preceded by *l* and followed by *p*. The segmentation is therefore /slijp-s/. In *slept*, *s*, *l*, and *p* are assigned to the initial form by Rule 1 as above; *t* is assigned to the final morph by Rule 2, *t* being a partial communis of Column D; and *e* falls under Rule 4 and is assigned to the initial morph. In *shook* /šuk/, *š* and *k* belong to the initial form by Rule 1 and *u* belongs to the final morph by Rule 2. In *hit* /hit/, *h*, *i*, and *t* all belong to the total communis of 5 and hence are part of the initial morph. The final morph is therefore zero. There are no merger phonemes in the present table.

The phonemic composition of morphs established through the rule of extension from a perfect square is determined without difficulty. Since the portion of the sequence derived from the square must be identical in phonemic composition (except for phonologic changes) with the sequence as it occurs in the square, the morph derived by extension is merely the remainder. Thus, in *huckleberry*, the division of which into two morphs is justified by the rule of extension, the final morph is /ˈberij/ as in *berry*:*berries*::*sofa*:*sofas*, and the remainder is /ˈhəkəl/.[5]

The semantically imperfect square follows the same rules as those described previously for the perfect square. They are applicable inasmuch as the procedure is purely formal and the semantic differences of the morphs play no role.

The formally imperfect square, in accordance with its definition, can contain only

5. There is a difference of stress here between *-berry* and *berry*, which is, however, phonologically regular.

forms with inflectional morphs. By putting the members of each of the various inflectional classes into one-to-one relationship with each other, an inflectional array is formed. Where, as in the earlier example based on *sleeps*, the extended array contains inflectional forms, the inflectional array contains the extended array as a part. Thus to the forms in Table 1 there are added the inflected forms of all verbs, including those with -/z/ or -/əz/ in Column A, and all the irregular forms. The same set of rules can be applied as for the perfect square based on the total and partial communis. The inflectional field which contains *man:men* will have two columns, one for singular forms and one for plural and a very large number of rows. Then /m-n/ will be the total communis of the row containing *man*, and /-æ-/ and /-e-/ will be the partial communis (in this case unique to each of the respective rows). The segmentation is therefore /m-n/ and /-æ-/ for the singular and /m-n/ and /-e-/ for the plural.

The rules for the assignment of morphs to the same morpheme can now be easily derived. In non-inflectional arrays all the initial morphs of the same row belong to the same morpheme, and all the final morphs of the same column belong to the same morpheme. For inflectional forms the same rules hold as applied in the entire inflectional field. For example, in Table 1, the morphs /slijp/- and /slep/- of line 1 belong to the same morpheme, and the morph -/iŋ/ of Column C constitutes a single-membered morpheme. These rules account for the morphs in perfect, semantically defective, and formally defective squares. In extensions the morph which occurs in a square as well as in the extended form is a member of the same morpheme. The morph *berry* in *berry* and *berries* belongs to the same morpheme as the *-berry* in *huckleberry*.[6]

The variations in phonemic composition between morphs of the same morpheme, sometimes called "allomorphs," are systematically stated in that portion of the grammar called "morphophonemics." The alternations of allomorphs may be divided into three types—phonologic, paradigmatic, and irregular. Where the choice of morph alternants is determined by a phoneme or phoneme sequence of the morph with which it is in construction, the alternation is said to be "phonologic." The alternation between the -/s/, -/z/, and -/əz/ 'morphs of the third person singular present of the verb in English is phonologic because the choice among them is dependent on the final phoneme of the noun stem, -/s/ following *p, t, k, f, þ;* -/z/ following *b, d, g, v, ð, m, n, ŋ, r, l* and vowels; and -/əz/ following *s, z, š, ž, č, j.* Paradigmatic alternation occurs when a morpheme in an inflectional array is connected by

6. Since phonologic regularity is required, the rules described here, while they will segment *duch-ess* into two morphs by the extension rule, will not allow us to identify the initial morph as belonging to the same morpheme as *duke*. It is difficult to establish any precise rule that would justify this common assumption. It could be established rather arbitrarily on a probability basis. In fact, the longer the form, the closer the phonetic resemblance, and the closer the meaning resemblance, the more convincing the identification becomes. Measures of semantic resemblance could be based on frequency of appearance in a body of text in the same context and phonetic resemblance on number of features shared. Then a combined index might be calculated. In practice, such morpheme identifications are made largely when there is historical justification and avoided where there is none.

perfect squares with other morphemes in parallel rows or parallel columns. Members of a restricted inflectional array are in paradigmatic alternation if there is any alternation at all. Referring again to Table 1, the alternation *keep* ~ *kep* is paradigmatic because it is connected by perfect squares to *weep* ~ *wep*, *sleep* ~ *slep*, etc. Such a set of morphemes forms a paradigmatic class. The well-known conjugational and declensional subclasses of Indo-European languages are examples of paradigmatic classes.

The final class of alternations consists of the irregular ones, members of formally imperfect squares, which are neither paradigmatically nor phonologically selected.

At a number of points in the foregoing analysis of the morpheme it was made clear that other alternative rules of procedure were possible. The particular choices made aimed at a consistent methodology which would approximate as closely as possible the actual practice of morphemic analysis in American linguistics. In one important respect, however, a quite different method might be suggested by which we approach more closely the viewpoint of the first chapter. We might modify one of the basic assumptions of morphemic analysis, namely, that of phonemic accountability, so that we no longer require every phoneme to belong to one morph only.[7] We allow sequences of one or more morphs and require merely that every phoneme belong to some sequence. Thus we are not obliged to decide whether the *-oo-*, -/u/-, of *took* /tuk/, belongs to the morpheme of "take" or that of the past, but assign all the phonemes to a morpheme sequence "take" + "past." In effect, this was what was done in the more old-fashioned statement that *took* is the past of *take* where no attempt is made at division into morphs. A systematic methodology for this approach can be constructed; all the members of a single row or a single column of an array are treated as a finite SS, and the variations of form in successive columns and rows are treated as one-to-one external transformations. For example, one finite SS will consist of all the present tense verb forms of English, and another of all past tenses. The two SS will be isomorphic and connected by a set of one-to-one transformations which carries each present form into a single past. The rules of transformation will include substitution, transposition, and set multiplication.[8] In this way, a procedure based on a standard form of mathematics can justify so-called "replacives," e.g., the substitution of *-oo-* in the past for *-a-* of the present in *take*, as a normal process, in place of its shadowy status alongside the segmentation method described earlier.

Throughout the preceding discussion the fundamental question was not raised concerning the unit which is to be employed in the squares which are basic to the method. In all the examples cited, the sequences from which segmentation started were words. Since one of the initial assumptions was that every word boundary is a morph boundary, while every morph boundary is not necessarily a word boundary, if we begin with words, we are sure of some morph boundaries at the start. The goal

7. It was seen that, because of merger and unassigned phonemes in irregular forms, this requirement cannot be carried out completely in any case.

8. See Appendix III, "The External Transformations of Sign Systems."

then becomes to determine how many morphs there are in each word, one being a permitted and frequent answer. It might seem that this requires the word to be exactly defined before morphological analysis can begin. In fact, this is not necessary. We need only be sure that the boundaries of the unit we start with are word boundaries, not that it is a single word, which would require an exact definition. Let us suppose that we start with a sequence of two words and that, in the absence of a definition of the word, we do not know how many words it contains. The use of a perfect square will immediately segment it into words, and, in accordance with the method outlined earlier, each part (now a word) will be investigated further for the possibility of further segmentation. If we did not know that *good cheese* was two words, the square *good cheese*:*good butter*: :*bad cheese*:*bad butter* would segment it into *good* and *cheese*, and we would proceed from there.

But how can we be sure that the units we use are single words or sequences of words, e.g., that the boundaries of our units are word boundaries? Since a basic presupposition of word analysis is that every expression contains an integral number of words, then the boundaries of every expression are necessarily word boundaries. In practice, we shall choose very short expressions which occur independently, in order to avoid a multiple series of segmentations before reaching the morph. This corresponds with actual practice. The linguist begins his morphological analysis with short sequences which are likely to be single words or a very short succession of words. This is typically true of items elicited as vocabulary, which are usually single-word utterances.

On the other hand, it might be thought that segmentation by successive applications of the method of squares, since it eventually reaches words, constitutes a definition of the word. This is not true because we do not know at what point we have reached a word as distinct from, say, a morpheme, a phrase, or a clause boundary, all of which are likewise word boundaries.

By the same token it will not be circular, since the definition of the word was not used in defining the morpheme, to start with the morpheme as delimited in this section and ask which sequences of morphs constitute words or, what comes to the same thing, which morph boundaries are also word boundaries. To do this is to define the word in terms of the morpheme and will be attempted in the next section.

THE WORD

The word as a unit occupies a paradoxical position in contemporary linguistic science. Such a unit, roughly coinciding in usage with its employment in everyday language and in the discourse of sciences other than linguistics, occurs almost universally in the actual practice of descriptive linguists as the dividing line between the two levels of morphological (infra-word) and syntactic (supra-word) constructions. Yet no generally accepted and satisfactory definition exists, and some linguists deny any validity to the word as a unit, relegating it to folk linguistics. Others believe that the word must be defined separately for each language and that there are probably some languages to which the concept is inapplicable. Some define the word in phonological terms, as, e.g., when a word in Czech is defined as a sequence with stress on its initial syllabic. Other definitions depend on the distribution of meaningful units and may be qualified as morphological or grammatical.[9] Here belongs Bloomfield's well-known definition of the word as the minimal free form. This definition has the advantage, lacking in so many others, of being operational. Unfortunately, it leads to some results not at all in agreement with the traditional notion, although it was manifestly intended to correspond at least approximately to the ordinary conception of the word. For example, *the* in English would not be a word but *the king of England's* in the sentence *the king of England's realm includes land on several continents* would. This is not in itself a fatal objection to its defining *some* unit, but it cannot be considered an adequate explication of ordinary usage.

Before proceeding with the definition proposed, we must ask what requirements must be fulfilled by a definition for it to be considered satisfactory. The popular conception of the word as indicated by the use of space or other devices in the orthographies of various languages is not sufficiently consistent to make possible a definition which will justify all existing practices. As generally in problems of scientific definition, we take the existing usage as a point of departure and one to which our results must, in general, conform. Among the requirements that must be satisfied for the definition of the word to correspond to the usual conception of this unit are the following: It should consist of a continuous sequence of phonemes such that every utterance in a language may be divided into a finite number of words exhaustively (i.e., with no phoneme unassigned to some word) and unambiguously (every phoneme should belong to some word). It would also be expected, as already indicated, that every word boundary should be a morph boundary, while some morph boundaries would be not word boundaries but intra-word boundaries.

To aid in the comprehension of what might otherwise appear a set of obscure maneuvers, an informal account of the nature of the solution will first be given. The continuity, or, as it is sometimes phrased, the non-interruptibility, of the word has been mentioned previously as one desideratum of a satisfactory definition. This suggests immediately that the word be defined simply as a non-interruptible unit, as a sequence within which another sequence cannot be inserted. However, it will soon appear that, while in general this is true, it does not suffice for a definition. For example, we can insert *r* in *gate* to get *grate*, but we wish *gate* to be a word in English. We can insert *house* in *schools* to obtain *schoolhouses*, but we would certainly want *schools* to be a word. The procedure is primarily motivated by the search for a unit at whose boundaries certain types of insertions occur if it coincides with a word boundary, which are not permitted when it is not such a boundary. The result is the determination of a unit, here called the "nucleus," consisting of one or more morphs and therefore intermediate between the morph and the word in length. For any utterance $m \geq n \geq w$, where m is the number of morphs, n the number of nuclei, and w the number of words. The nucleus having been determined, all nucleus

9. For a convenient review of the history of the subject see Knud Togeby, "Qu'est-ce qu'un mot?" *Travaux du Cercle linguistique de Copenhague*, V (1949), 97–111.

boundaries can be tested to discover whether they are word boundaries. Unlimited possible insertion of nuclei at a nucleus boundary makes it a word boundary. Since this procedure gives us word boundaries and since words are then defined simply as stretches between word boundaries, the requirement of continuity is necessarily fulfilled.

Another feature of the procedure which perhaps deserves preliminary explanation is that it is analytic in the sense of the first chapter. That is, starting from some one expression, we seek to analyze it by what are, in effect—although a purely linguistic terminology is utilized at this point—horizontal and vertical transformations by means of which the structure of the construction is determined. We do not ask, as is sometimes done, whether *hand* is a word in English but rather whether, in the expression *the hand is quicker than the eye*, the sequence *hand* constitutes a word. This is, among other reasons, because in many   es we want a sequence, e.g., Latin *trans*, to be a word as the preposition meaning *across* in *coelum non mentem mutant qui trans mare vehunt*, but to be part of a word when compounded with a verb, as in *sic transit gloria mundi*. The same sequence *trans* in these two examples belongs to different classes, i.e., has different horizontal transformations. It will be recalled that, in the discussion of subconstructions and constructions in the previous chapter, the constituents were restricted classes. The decision as to whether a particular sequence of phonemes is a word, therefore, comes as an incidental result of answering the question whether the particular class to which it belongs is a word class in the construction in which it appears.

We start with the morph substitution class (MSC) in terms of which it will be possible to define the key nucleus unit referred to earlier. An MSC is a set of morphs which belong to the same restricted class and may substitute for some morph in the expression to be analyzed. For example, in the expression *the singer broke the contract*, the morph *sing-* of *singer* belongs to an MSC which contains *sing-*, *play-*, *min-*, and other members, since *the player broke the contract* and *the miner broke the contract* are both expressions of the language. However, *re-form* does not belong to the MSC of *sing-* because it consists of two morphs. It is easy to see that the MSC is simply the set of either initial or final morphs in the columns or rows, respectively, of an extended array as defined in the discussion of the morpheme.

The differing methods for defining the morpheme will have practically no effect on the end result. The only exception is the type of discontinuous morpheme described by Harris in his "Discontinuous Morphemes" and not considered among the possible alternatives in the earlier discussion.[10] Such a procedure is naturally excluded, since such discontinuous elements violate the requirement of continuity enunciated at the outset.

Most disputed cases of morph division involve combinations, such as *huckleberry*, in which one or both of the elements belong to such a small and unique MSC that nothing can be inserted anyway, so that either solution, as one morph or as two morphs, leads to the same end result.

10. Zellig Harris, "Discontinuous Morphemes," *Language*, XXI (1945), 121–27.

The next notion to be defined is that of a thematic sequence. In the example of *sing-er* earlier, it was seen that *re-form-*, although a sequence of two morphs and representing two MSC's in its substitution behavior, was like a single MSC, that containing *sing-*, *play-*, etc. A sequence of two or more MSC's will be said to constitute a "thematic sequence" if (1) there is some single MSC for which it may always substitute and give a grammatical utterance and (2) none of the MSC's is equivalent to, that is, has exactly the same membership as, the single MSC for which the sequence may substitute. The thematic sequence may be said to form a theme and to be an expansion of the single MSC it can replace. Thematic expansion includes both what is usually called "derivation" and what is called "compounding." Thus *duck-ling* is a sequence of two morphs which is called a "derivational construction." It consists of a representative of the MSC which contains *duck-*, *gos-*, etc., and the MSC which contains *-ling*. It may substitute for the single MSC containing *hen*, *chicken*, *goose*, etc., among its members, and neither of the MSC's making up the thematic sequence is equivalent in membership to this latter class, since both contain members *gos-*, *-ling*, etc., not found in the MSC of *hen*, *chicken*, etc.

We are now ready to define "nucleus." A nucleus is either (1) a single MSC which is not part of a thematic sequence or (2) a thematic sequence consisting of MSC's. Among single MSC's are some which are expandable into thematic sequences but are not thus expanded in the particular expression analyzed, and some which are not. In the sentence *the farmer killed the ugly duckling*, there are nine morphs: (1) *the*, (2) *farm-*, (3) *-er*, (4) *kill-*, (5) *-ed*, (6) *the*, (7) *ugly*, (8) *duck-*, (9) *-ling*. There are seven nuclei: (1) *the* (a non-expandable MSC); (2) *farm-er* (a thematic expansion consisting of two MSC's); (3) *kill-* (a single MSC expandable, e.g., into *un-hook-*); (4) *-ed* (a non-expandable MSC); (5) *the* [as in (1)]; (6) *ugly* (a single MSC expandable, e.g., into *un-love-able*); (7) *duck-ling* (a thematic sequence containing two MSC's).

There remains, finally, the distinction between nucleus boundaries that are also word boundaries and those which are not. A nucleus boundary is an infra-word boundary if there is a maximum to the number of nuclei that can be inserted. Often this maximum is zero, that is, nothing can be inserted. It is a boundary between words in the other instances, that is, where there is no maximum to the number of insertions of nuclei, if there is "infinite" insertion.

In the foregoing sentence no nucleus can be inserted between (3) *kill-* and (4) *-ed;* therefore, it is not a word boundary. Between all the others insertions without limit may be made. Thus between (1) *the* and (2) *farmer* we can insert *very headstrong, cruel, ruthless*, etc.; between (2) *farmer* and (3) *kill-* can be inserted *who lives in the house which is on the road which leads into the highway which had been damaged by rainstorms*, etc.

There is one kind of insertion which must be forbidden by a special rule, since it can be carried out without limit at any nucleus boundary whatever. The forbidden insertion consists of one whose initial nucleus is the same as the nucleus following the boundary and whose final nucleus is the same as the nucleus before the boundary.

In the foregoing sentence, we might insert between (4) *kill-* and (5) *-ed* the nuclei *-ed* and *slaughter-* to produce: *the farmer killed and slaughtered the ugly duckling*; but *-ed*, the initial morph of the inserted, belongs to the same nucleus as (5) *-ed*, and *slaughter-* is a member of the same nucleus as (4) *kill-*.

It is understood that no insertion is legitimate unless it leaves unchanged the restricted class of the morphemes preceding and following the insertion, since we are operating with classes throughout. Thus, to insert as follows between *kill-* and *-ed* in the foregoing sentence is not permitted: *The farmer kill- (-ing the other animals spar-) -ed the ugly duckling.* This is forbidden because in the original sentence the restricted class of *kill-* is that of all preterite verb stems in English with pasts in *-d*, whereas the preceding insertion transforms it into the restricted class containing all present stems. These two classes have a different membership. For example, *take-* belongs to the latter but not the former. Another way of stating this is to say that no insertion is allowed which changes the restricted construction as defined in the first chapter.

Phoneme modifications at word boundary, often known as word *sandhi*, if regular, make no difference to the analysis. Whenever the modification can be stated in terms of phonemes, that is, is phonologically regular, the result is merely to restrict the insertion at the boundary to a subclass which begins with a particular set of phonemes. But the subtraction of an infinite enumerable set from another infinite enumerable set still leaves an infinite enumerable set. The exclusion of all odd integers from the whole set of integers still leaves the infinite set of even integers. The *sandhi* alternation in English between *a* and *an* means that insertion without limit is still possible between *an* and *apple*, but the first adjective must begin with a vowel.

There is one rare type of *sandhi* phenomenon in which the *sandhi* gives rise to a single phoneme in place of the final phoneme of the preceding nucleus and the initial phoneme of the following one. For example, in Sanskrit if a nucleus ends in basic *-n* and the next begins with basic *l-*, the result is a single phoneme $\tilde{l}$, a nasalized lateral. In this case the number of words is determinate, but the ascription of $\tilde{l}$ to the former or latter word is arbitrary. If we changed our phonemic analysis to make $\tilde{}$ a separate phoneme, we could divide *l* into two phonemes and assign $\tilde{}$ to the former word and *l* to the latter. A similar analysis applies to junctural phonemes if they are part of a phonemic description. If they are treated like ordinary segmental phonemes and assigned a position between the two phonemes which immediately precede and follow the juncture, the number of words is definite, but the assignment of the juncture to either word is arbitrary.

The present procedure resolves the contradiction between phonological and grammatical definitions of the word. In the former it is not the presence of stress or some other marker which demarcates the word, a point of view which sometimes leads to strange results,[11] but the existence of stress or other *variation* which pro-

11. To take one instance, in Polish the vast majority of words have penultimate stress, but there are exceptions. If we defined the word by this stress pattern, *Améryka* would consist of a

duces different classes whose analyses by the present distributional (grammatical) method often establishes word boundaries.

For example, in Latin, what is usually called a word is stressed on the penultimate syllable if this is long (i.e., has a short vowel followed by a consonant, or a long vowel) and on the antepenultimate if the penultimate is short. This suggests a phonological definition of the word unit based on the rule of stress. A distributional analysis gives the same result. For example, the enclitic *-que*, "and," is reckoned as a syllable with the immediately preceding sequence in locating the stress which serves as the means of discovering word boundaries under a phonologic definition. Thus, by the traditional phonologic definition, *dóminus*, "lord," and *dominúsque*, "and the lord," are both one word. Under the present purely distributional analysis, likewise, *dominúsque* will be one word and not two. In *sérvus dominúsque venêrunt*, "the slave and the master came," *domin-ús-que* consists of three nuclei. The nucleus of *domin-* has as other members *lēgāt-*, *serv-*, etc., and all other stress-shifted noun themes which may be substituted for *domin-* in this expression. Nothing can be inserted either between this nucleus and that of *-ús-* or that of *-ús-* and that of *-que, -ve,* and other enclitics. Hence these are not word boundaries, and *dominúsque* is a single word. In *dóminus vēnit*, "the lord came," *dómin-us* has two nuclei which are not equivalent to any of the three in *dominúsque*, since the class of *dómin-(us)* contains *lēgāt-*, *sérv-*, *dómin-*, etc., and not *lēgāt-*, *serv-*, *domin-*, and *-us* is not phonemically identical with *-ús*. Here also no nucleus can be inserted between that of *dómin-* and *-us*, and its analysis as a single word results.

The reason that the nucleus is required as a unit rather than the morph, as the basis for an infinite insertion rule, is that in a few languages like Eskimo there is indefinite derivational expansion. If the morph were our unit, the possibility of infinite insertion within such derivational sequences of morphs would make each morph boundary a word boundary, and our results would not at all correspond to the usual idea of a word in these languages. Since the entire sequence of classes of derivational morphs can be substituted for a single root MSC to which no one of them is equivalent, the entire indefinite expansion is a single nucleus and therefore within the same word.

As defined here, the nucleus is a unit of which there is always a fixed number in the class of words which are mutually substitutable in the same construction. As such it agrees with the notion of fixed positions in the word developed by Boas in connection with the description of American Indian languages.

In terms of the general grammar of sign systems as developed in the first chapter, the word in those languages which, unlike Eskimo, do not have patterns of infinite word derivation is to be identified with the sequence in sign systems with sequences distinct from elements and which are of finite sequence order, that is, have a finite number of sequences made up from the elements. In both cases there is only

---

"word" *Améry*, and *ka* would belong to the next word. In the analysis proposed below, *Améryka* is a sequence in the same class of nuclei as any Polish noun with penultimate stress, and, since nothing can be inserted between the stem (*Améryk-*) and the inflectional nucleus (*-a*), it is one word.

one unit such that insertion without limit of members of this unit at the boundary between any succession of two of them is possible. What we are asserting is that, given a language of this type without meanings, that is, in an uninterpreted specified system, the analytic methods of the first chapter would lead to exactly the same successions of phonemes which are words by the procedure of the present section being interpreted as the sequences which are the members of constructions. The phonemes, of course, would be the elements.

In languages of the type of Eskimo there are two units which allow of infinite insertion, one being within the word and the other being the word. In the same manner, in a sign system with an infinite number of different sequences, there must be some rule for making up an unlimited number of sequences out of elements, as well as the rules for building constructions of indefinite length with sequences as the members. The first unit capable of indefinite expansion is therefore within the sequence, and the second is the sequence itself. Hence in languages of the Eskimo type analytic procedures applied to the language as an uninterpreted sign system will isolate sequences which will coincide with the words of Eskimo and infra-sequential units which are expandable subunits within the word. Hence the sequence corresponds to the word in either type of language. Eskimo, which has 18 phonemes, is therefore of element order 18 and sequence order ∞ and would be symbolized in the notation of the first chapter as an L_∞^{18}.

The subsequence is to be identified with the nucleus generally, but sometimes with the MSC. For convenience of exposition, the examples of the latter portion of the first chapter will be repeated.

CASE 1. INFLECTION

I. A, AB, ABB, ABBB . . .
II. C, CB', CB'B', CB'B'B' . . .

Here the communis of B and B' is the stem, and the propriae are inflections. Each of these is a nucleus, for our test of inflection was a one-to-one correspondence of the members of a class which appears in one construction with the members of a class which appears in another. Hence there are no substitutable members left over in either class such that the succession consisting of the communis of B and B' and the propria of B in I or B' in II could substitute for it. If this were possible, then B or B' would be a theme divisible into two MSC's.

The one-to-one correspondence between members of B and B' can be carried out only in an uninterpreted system if the forms are all phonologically or paradigmatically regular. Therefore, not all nuclei of inflectional arrays occurring in languages can be identified with the subsequences of this model in uninterpreted systems, and there is need for two different terms.

CASE 2. AGREEMENT

I. BC,|BCC, BCD|,|BCCC, BCCD, BCDD| . . .
II. B'C',|B'C'C', B'C'D|,|B'C'C'C', B'C'C'D, B'C'DD|. . .

The analysis here is similar to the preceding. The communis of B and B' and of C and C' are stem nuclei, and the propriae are inflectional nuclei.

CASE 3. EXOCENTRIC DERIVATION

I. A, AB, ABB, ABBB ...

II. C, CD, CDD, CDDD ...

$$(D = B' + K)$$

Here the communis of B and B' is a stem nucleus. The propria of B is an inflective nucleus. The propria of B' is a derivational morpheme which is part of an expanded nucleus, which also contains the stem nucleus of the communis of B and B'. The class K is simply a word class not susceptible of further analysis.

CASE 4. ENDOCENTRIC DERIVATION

I. A, AD, ADD ...

$$(D = B + B')$$

The communis of B and B' is a stem nucleus. The propriae are likewise nuclei of regular derivation. The forms of Class D, unlike those of Class D of the exocentric construction, consist of a sequence of two nuclei, since there is no single word class for which they can substitute.

CHAPTER III

GENETIC RELATIONSHIP AMONG LANGUAGES

THE establishment of valid hypotheses concerning genetic relationships among languages is a necessary preliminary to the systematic reconstruction of their historical development. The appropriate techniques cannot be applied to languages chosen at random but only if preliminary-investigation has already indicated the likelihood of the success of such an enterprise. Correct hypotheses of relationship are also of very real significance to the archeologist, the physical anthropologist, the ethnologist, and the culture historian, even in those instances in which systematic linguistic reconstruction has not yet begun and may, indeed, in our present state of descriptive knowledge be of only limited feasibility. The considerations advanced in this chapter are intended as a realistic analysis of the factors involved in the formulation of reliable hypotheses of such relationships. It should be possible, through clarification of the assumptions involved, to resolve the conflicting classifications found in certain areas. It is likewise hoped that a sufficient basis will be presented so that the non-specialist can intelligently evaluate alternative classifications through an independent examination of the linguistic evidence itself.

Hypotheses concerning genetic relationship among languages are established by comparing languages. But languages are complex wholes which exhibit many facets, and the question which inevitably arises at the outset is one of relevance. Are all aspects of language equally germane for comparison? A language contains a set of meaningful forms (morphemes), themselves composed of meaningless sound types (phonemes) and entering into various combinations in accordance with the rules of its grammar. The meaningful forms (morphemes) may themselves be roots, in which case they are normally assigned to the lexicon, or non-roots (affixes) with derivational or inflectional grammatical function, in which case their description is part of the grammar. In either instance they involve both sound and meaning.

It is clear that, in principle, the connection between sound and meaning is arbitrary, in the sense that any meaning can be represented by any combination of sounds. A dog may as easily be called *Hund*, *cane*, *sabaka*, or *kalb* and, in fact, is—in German, Italian, Russian, and Arabic, respectively. Moreover, the thousands of meaningful forms of any language are basically independent. Except for the occasional avoidance of homonyms, which involves an exceedingly small limitation, the principle holds in general that, just because you call a dog a "dog," it does not mean you have to call a cat a "cat." It is unlikely, however, that you will call it a "dog." From these two principles of the arbitrariness of the sound-meaning connection and the independence of meaningful forms, it follows that resemblances beyond chance in both form and meaning require a historical explanation, whether through borrowing or through common origin.

By "lexical resemblance" will be meant similarity in sound and meaning of root morphemes—e.g., English 'hænd and German 'hant, both meaning "hand." By "grammatical resemblance" will be meant similarity of both sound and meaning in non-root morphemes, e.g., English -ər and German -ər, both indicating the comparative of adjectives. Both lexical and grammatical resemblances thus defined are relevant as evidence for historical relationships. On the other hand, similarity in meaning not accompanied by similarity in sound or similarity in sound without corresponding similarity in meaning may be considered of negligible value. Thus the presence of sex gender expressed by morphemes without phonetic resemblance or the existence of tonal systems without specific form-meaning similarities in the forms employing tones should be excluded as arguments for historical connection.

The order of meaningful elements may be considered a formal characteristic, like sound. In syntactic constructions only two possibilities usually occur in the arrangement of forms, A either preceding or following B, as contrasted with the numerous possibilities of sound combinations. Hence arguments based on word order are of minor significance. This is all the more so because the kinds of constructional meaning which may be significant are necessarily small, e.g., dependent genitive or actor-action. Historically unconnected occurrences of such resemblances are therefore extremely likely and heavily documented.

The order and meaning of morpheme classes within complex words in certain cases offer far greater combinational possibilities. The meaning possibilities involved are more numerous than for syntactic construction, though less than for sound-meaning resemblances. For example, within the verb complex we may have such meaning categories as pronominal subject, direction of action relative to speaker, tense, transitivity or non-transitivity, etc. This method can be used with real effect only in polysynthetic languages, those with complex internal word structure. Moreover, lack of agreement in such matters is not significant where sufficient specific sound-meaning agreements in morphemes are found. For example, the verb structures of Russian and Hindustani are quite different; once the periphrastic construction based on the participles became established, the whole elaborate inherited inflectional mechanism of the Indic verb was eliminated at one stroke. Even where such agreements are found among polysynthetic languages, it would seem to provide merely confirmation, however welcome, of results also attainable by the more generally applicable method of morpheme comparison.

Granted that sound-meaning similarities of morphemes weigh most significantly in determining historic relationships, it is evident that not all such resemblances need stem from historic factors. Thus Didinga, a language of the Anglo-Egyptian Sudan, has badh in the meaning "bad" and man means "man" in Korean. Moreover, although, as stated previously, the connection between sound and meaning is arbitrary, that is, unpredictable, there does exist in certain instances a well-marked tendency far greater than chance association between certain sounds and meanings. Examples are the nursery words for "mother" and "father" and onomatopoetic terms. This factor will increase slightly the number of sound-meaning resemblances between any two languages. If we call this source of resemblance "symbolism," then there are four classes of causes for sound-meaning resemblances, two of which—chance and symbolism—are non-historic, while the remaining two—genetic relationship and borrowing—involve historic processes.[1]

The two basic methodologic processes then become the elimination of chance and symbolism leading to hypotheses of historic connections and the segregation of those instances in which borrowing is an adequate explanation from those on which genetic relationship must be posited.

The most straightforward method of eliminating chance would be the calculation of the expected number of chance resemblances between two languages, taking into account their respective phonemic structures. In practice, this proves extremely difficult, and no satisfactory technique for its accomplishment has yet been devised. Moreover, it requires, in addition to consideration of the possibilities of phonemic combination, a frequency weighting of phonemes. If both languages show, as is normal, considerable variation in the frequency of the various phonemes and if similar phonemes are among the most frequent in each language, the over-all expectation of chance coincidences is increased. More practicable would be a percentage count of resemblances among large numbers of pairs of presumably unrelated languages. This would also have the advantage of taking into account resemblances due to symbolism also. Where the percentage of resemblance between languages is very high, say 20 per cent or more, some historic factor, whether borrowing or genetic relationship, must be assumed. Where the proportion of similarities is significantly lower, a consideration of the qualitative characteristics of the sound-meaning resemblances found and the broadening of the basis of comparison to other languages, usually numerous, which show resemblances to the pair being considered (mass comparison) bring into play factors of the highest significance which should always insure a decisive answer. These factors quite overshadow the mere percentage of resemblances. In many instances this, if small, may be approximately the same between several pairs of languages, yet in some cases there will be certainty of historic relationship beyond any reasonable doubt and in some others no compelling reason to accept such an explanation.

Qualitatively, not all sound-meaning similarities are of equal value as evidence for a historical connection. For example, the longer a form, the less likely does it become that chance is an explanation. From this point of view, "*intər'našənəl* in language A and *intərnatsjo'nal* in language B is far more likely the result of historic factors than are -*k*, "locative," in language A and -*g*, "locative," in language B.

The natural unit of interlingual comparison is the morpheme with its alternant morphs.[2] The presence of similar morph alternants in similar environments is of very

1. Further complex causes, involving certain combinations of these four fundamental causes, will be discussed in the following chapter on "The Problems of Linguistic Subgrouping."

2. In addition to the morpheme as the fundamental unit of interlanguage comparison, resemblances below the morphemic level involving units that might be called "submorphs" are also the result of genetic relationship. The following example will help to indicate what is meant. In cer-

great significance as an indication of historical connection, normally genetic relationship. This is particularly so if the alternation is irregular, especially if suppletive, that is, entirely different. The English morpheme with alternants *gud-*, *bet-*, *be-*, with the morph alternant *bet-* occurring before *-ər*, "comparative," and the alternant *be-* before *-st*, "superlative," corresponds in form and conditions of alternation with German *gu:t-*, *bes-*, *be-*, with *bes-* occurring before *-ər*, "comparative," and *be-* before *-st*, "superlative." We have here not only the probability that a similar form is found in the meaning "good" but that it shows similar and highly arbitrary alternations before the representatives of the comparative and superlative morphemes. The likelihood that all this is the result of chance is truly infinitesimal.

Similar rules of combinability, even without alternations in form, are also of considerable significance. In Niger-Congo languages, not only are forms similar to *to* in the meaning "ear" found widely, but they are also found in construction with the same classificational affix *ku*.

Such indications of historical connection founded on morphological irregularities of form and combinability may not always be found. Many languages of isolating or of highly regular structure will have few or no morph alternants. Even where originally present, they are subject to constant analogical pressure toward replacement by regular alternations. Hence their chance of survival in related languages is not great. Where they are found, however, they are precious indexes of historical relationships.

Another factor bearing on the value of particular resemblances is semantic plausibility. This is greatest where the meanings are similar enough to have been given as translation equivalents for the same term in some third, usually European, language or for translation equivalents in two other languages. Semantic plausibility likewise attaches to comparisons involving single-step, widely attested shifts in meaning, e.g., "moon" and "month." The more intermediate semantic steps allowed, the larger the chance of obtaining form-meaning similarity, some of which may indeed stem from historical connection. But the greater the methodological latitude permitted, the less plausible is each individual comparison.

Considerations derived from the extension of comparison beyond the pair of languages initially considered are of fundamental importance. The problem as to whether the resemblances between two languages are merely the result of chance plus symbolism can then be subjected to further and decisive tests. Let us say that, as is usually the case, one or more other languages or language groups resemble the two languages in question. The following fundamental probability considerations

---

tain languages of the Adamawa group of Niger-Congo languages, as a survival of a noun suffix *-ma* used with names of indefinitely divisible substances, e.g., water, fat, a far larger than chance number of nouns with meanings of this sort end in *-ma* or *-m*, depending on the languages. However, there is no class system involving plural formation or adjective or noun agreement, as in other Niger-Congo languages. The methodology of chap. ii would not lead to the analysis of this element as a morpheme in a synchronic description of these languages. Such cases are marginal and too infrequent to be anything but a reinforcement of what is provable by normal morpheme comparison.

apply. The likelihood of finding a resemblance in sound and meaning in three languages is the square of its probability in two languages. In general, the probability for a single language must be raised to the $(n - 1$th) power for n languages. Thus if five languages each showed a total of 8 per cent sound-meaning resemblance to one another, on a chance basis one would expect $(0.08)^4$ or 0.00004096 resemblances in all five languages. This is approximately 1/25,000. In other words, were one to compare sets of one thousand forms from all five languages, one would have to do this twenty-five times before a single instance of a resemblance in all five languages would occur. Even recurrence in three languages would be rare on a chance basis, 0.0064, that is, less than 1 per cent. Hence the presence of a fair number of recurrent sound-meaning resemblances in three, four, or more languages is a certain indication of historical connection.

Finally, there are considerations based on the phonetic form. The presence of recurrent, i.e., non-unique correspondences, adds greatly to the value of the comparison. In this area, also, mass comparison is of significance. Are the forms found in a number of languages such as to suggest that they are changed forms of a common original? The bringing-in of closely related languages on each side will then show tentative reconstructions converging as we go back in time. This procedure is not possible where only two languages are being compared.

Assuming that the factors just cited lead to the establishment of a historical connection, there still remains the problem of whether the resemblances in question can be explained by borrowing. While in particular and infrequent instances the question of borrowing may be doubtful, it is always possible to tell whether a mass of resemblances between two languages is the result of borrowing. A basic consideration is the a priori expectation and the historical documentation of the thesis that borrowing in culture words is far more frequent than in fundamental vocabulary and that derivational, inflectional, and pronominal morphemes and morph alternations are the least subject of all to borrowing. While it cannot be said that any single item might not on occasion be borrowed, fundamental vocabulary is proof against mass borrowing. The presence of fundamental vocabulary resemblances and resemblances in items with grammatical function, particularly if recurrent through a number of languages, is a sure indication of genetic relationship. Where a mass of resemblances is due to borrowing, they will tend to appear in cultural vocabulary and to cluster in certain semantic areas which reflect the cultural nature of the contact, and the resemblances will point toward one or, at most, two or three languages as donors. The forms will be too similar to those found in these particular languages, considering the great differences in other respects and the consequent historic remoteness of the relationship, if it really existed. Thus the Romance loanwords in English are almost all close to the French forms, in addition to hardly penetrating the basic vocabulary of English. Were English really a Romance language, it would show roughly equal similarities to all the Romance languages.

The presence of recurrent sound correspondences is not in itself sufficient to exclude borrowing as an explanation. Where loans are numerous, they often show such correspondences; thus French loanwords in English often show Fr. š = Eng. č, Fr. ã = Eng. œn (šās:čœns; šāt:čœnt; šɛ:z:čejr, etc.).

All these principles are well illustrated from Thai, whose resemblances to Chinese are the result of borrowing rather than genetic relationship, as is being realized more and more. Most of the resemblances usually cited between Thai and Sino-Tibetan languages, such as the existence of a tonal system, involve sound only or meaning only and are therefore irrelevant. The specific resemblances found with Sino-Tibetan languages always occur in forms found in Chinese, usually to the exclusion of other Sino-Tibetan languages. The specific form, even when found elsewhere, is always very close to Chinese. Moreover, the resemblances cluster in a few semantic spheres, the numerals from 2 to 10 and a few names of metals and domestic animals. In contrast, the Thai resemblances to the Kadai languages and Malayo-Polynesian tend to recur throughout the family, not just in some single language; are basic; do not concentrate in any particular semantic area; and exhibit an independence of form which excludes any particular Kadai or Malayo-Polynesian language as a source.

Borrowing can never be an over-all explanation of a mass of recurrent basic resemblances in many languages occurring over a wide geographical area. It is sometimes adduced in this *ad hoc* fashion. Since we find independent sets of resemblances between every pair of languages, among every group of three languages, and so on, each language would have to borrow from every other. A thesis of borrowing to account for resemblances must be speci 'c, pointing out which peoples have borrowed from which, and it must be plausible in terms of the factors just cited. It may be added that the vast majority of languages do not display mass borrowing, and, where it does occur, it is easily detected.

The method for discovering valid relationships described here may be summarized as resting on two main principles—the relevancy of form-meaning resemblances in morphemes to the exclusion of those based on form only and meaning only and the technique of group comparison of languages. Some of the reasons for this latter emphasis have been adduced earlier. There are further considerations which recommend this procedure. Instead of comparing a few or even just two languages chosen at random and for linguistically extraneous reasons, we proceed systematically by first comparing closely related languages to form groups with recurrent significant resemblances and then compare these groups with other similarly constituted groups. Thus it is far easier to see that the Germanic languages are related to the Indo-Aryan languages than that English is related to Hindustani. In effect, we have gained historic depth by comparing each group as a group, considering only those forms as possessing the likelihood of being original which are distributed in more than one branch of the group and considering only those etymologies as favoring the hypothesis of relationship in which tentative reconstruction brings the forms closer together. Having noted the relationship of the Germanic and Indo-Aryan languages, we bring in other groups of languages, e.g., Slavonic and Italic. In this process we determine with ever increasing definiteness the basic lexical and grammatical morphemes in regard to both phonetic form and meaning. On the other hand, we also see more easily that the Semitic languages and Basque do not belong to this aggregation of languages. Confronted by some isolated language without near congeners, we compare it with this general Indo-European rather than at random with single languages. It is a corollary of the considerations advanced here that if a language has no close relatives, it is more difficult to find its distant relatives. Therefore, we should begin with well-defined groups of more closely related languages and leave such isolated cases to be considered after more widespread families have been constituted. Table 2 will show that it is not mere percentage of resemblances between pairs of languages which is decisive, except for quite close relationships, but rather the setting-up of restricted groups of related languages which then enter integrally into more distant comparisons.

TABLE 2

	A	B	C	D	E	F	G	H	I
Head....	kar	kar	se	kal	tu	tu	to	fi	pi
Eye.....	min	ku	min	miŋ	min	aš	min	idi	iri
Nose....	tor	tör	ni	tol	was	waš	was	ik	am
One.....	mit	kan	kan	kaŋ	ha	kan	ken	he	čak
Two.....	ni	ta	ne	kil	ne	ni	ne	gum	gun
Blood...	kur	sem	sem	šam	i	sem	sem	fik	pix

In examining the forms in Table 2, the hypothesis immediately arises that A, B, C, and D form a related group of languages. We will call this "Group I." It is also apparent that E, F, and G constitute another related group (Group II), and that H and I are likewise connected (Group III). The hypothesis will also suggest itself that Groups I and II are related. On the other hand, the material cited offers no real support for the relationship of Group III to Groups I and II. If we look more closely, however, we will see that languages B and E show no likely cognates, whereas E has a form for "one," *ha*, closely resembling *he* in language H. E therefore shows a higher percentage resemblance to H than to B on the basis of isolated comparison. Yet the hypothesis that E is related to H rather than to B would hardly occur as a realistic one when all the relevant evidence from languages more closely related to E, B, and H is taken into consideration. The tables of percentages of resemblances among pairs of languages which are sometimes cited as evidence can at times be quite misleading, nor can elaborate statistical manipulations of these quantitative data add to their validity.

There is the further consideration that isolated hypotheses are less significant in their culture-historical implications and may even, on occasions, lead to erroneous conclusions. Thus it is no doubt true that Albanian, Bengali, and Swedish are related; but if all the intervening languages are unclassified or stated to be independent, some rather questionable historical deductions would be made. In addition, isolated hypotheses may lead to fruitless controversies, in which both parties have correct but only partial answers. Thus in aboriginal South America, where widespread relationships on a scale hitherto unrecognized actually exist, there are controversies which, transposed in terms of the Eurasian area, might run somewhat as follows. One investigator states that Albanian is related to Greek. The other disagrees and maintains, on the contrary, that it is related to Italian. Both present fairly convincing cases, since their hypotheses are correct, though, of course, a far stronger case could be presented for Indo-European as a whole, with the positions of Greek, Italian, and Albanian defined within it. Other linguists viewing the controversy either come to the cynical conclusion that, with sufficient effort, you can present a convincing case for any relationship, real or fancied, or decide that we need several more generations to gather the data necessary to decide the controversy.

As a heuristic principle, the swiftest and surest method of bringing into play many of the considerations discussed here is the compilation of comparative fundamental vocabularies of all the languages of an extended area. This accomplishes a number of purposes simultaneously. It involves the aspect of language least subject to borrowing outside grammatical elements. The forms are generally of fair length. Semantic straightforwardness is attained by using the translation equivalent of the same term in English or whatever language is used as the language of translation. The tendency of similar forms to appear in a number of languages, as well as the plausibility of descent from a common original, can easily be noted. The presence of recurrent phonetic correspondences can be seen without great difficulty. If, as is often the case, word lists or dictionaries include noun plurals or other morphological facts, even details of morphological combinations and alternations can be taken into account. Most important of all, perhaps, is that, where more than one family is represented, as is always the case when the languages examined are from an extensive area, the contrast between the relatively numerous and qualitatively superior resemblances among related languages, compared to the sporadic and qualitatively poorer resemblances among unrelated languages, becomes readily apparent. In this way the presence of unrelated languages provides a control for distinguishing mere chance from genetically significant resemblances.

A relationship may sometimes be first suggested by agreement in some strikingly irregular morphological alternation or very full agreement in some set of grammatical affixes. For example, I was first led to entertain the hypothesis of the relation of Zaghawa to Kanuri and Teda, to form the Central Saharan family, by a remarkable agreement in a conjugational paradigm in which the morphemes of the first two persons were suffixed while those of the third person were prefixed. All the personal affixes were, moreover, phonetically similar. An examination of the fundamental vocabulary of these languages, which followed, amply confirmed the result. As a general procedure, however, the great advantage of vocabulary is the large number of essentially independent items it furnishes which are comparable from language to language and which are always present. Moreover, where little information is available about languages, the data are far more likely to be lexical than grammatical. All available grammatical information should be systematically examined, but vocabulary leads most swiftly to the correct hypotheses as a general rule. The effectiveness of mass comparison of basic vocabulary, for all its apparent simplicity, is illustrated in Table 3 by only a few forms from all the contemporary languages of Europe.[3]

Note that, even by the time the second word has been examined, the correct hypothesis emerges. The subsequent words fully confirm the initial hypothesis again and again. I believe that it is not generally realized how great is the number of different ways in which a given number of languages can be genetically classified. If, for example, there are four languages, A, B, C, and D, the following classifications are

TABLE 3

	One	Two	Three	Head	Eye	Ear	Nose	Mouth	Tooth
Breton....	ünan	dau	tri	penn	lagad	skuarn	fri	genu	dant
Irish......	öːn	dɔː	tri	kjan	suːlʲ	kluəs	srɔːn	bjal	fjakalʲ
Welsh.....	ɨn	daɨ	tri	pen	hləgad	klɨst	truɨn	keg	dant
Danish. ..	en	toː?	treː?	hoːdhə	ɔjə	oːrə	nɛːsə	mon?	tan?
Swedish...	en	tvo	tre	hüvud	öga	öra	näsa	mun	tand
Dutch....	eːn	tveː	driː	hoːft	oːx	oːr	nöːs	mont	tant
English...	wən	tuw	*thr*ij	hed	aj	ihr	nowz	maw*th*	tuw*th*
German...	ajns	tsvaj	draj	kopf	augə	oːr	naːze	munt	tsaːn
French....	œ, yn	dö	trwa	teːt	œl/jö	oreːj	ne	buːš	dã
Italian....	uno, una	due	tre	testa	əkkjo	orekkjo	naso	bokka	dɛnte
Spanish...	un, una	dos	tres	kabesa	oxo	orexa	naso	boka	diente
Rumanian.	un	doj	trej	kap	okiu	ureke	nas	gurə	dinte
Albanian..	nʲə	du	tre	kokə	sü	vesh	hundə	goja	dhəmp
Greek.....	enas	dhjo	tris	kefáli	máti	aftí	míti	stóma	dhóndi
Lithuanian.	vienas	du	triːs	galva	akis	ausis	nosis	burna	dantis
Latvian...	viens	divi	triːs	galva	atss	auss	deguns	mute	zobs
Polish.....	jeden	dva	tši	glova	oko	uxo	nos	usta, gẽba	zõp
Czech.....	jeden	dva	tři	hlava	oko	uxo	nos	usta	zup
Russian...	adʲinˑ	dva, dvʲe	trʲi	galavá	óko	úxo	nos	rot	zup
Bulgarian .	edin	dva	tri	glava	oko	uxo	nos	usta	zəb
Serbo-Croatian ...	jedan	dva	tri	glava	oko	uho	nos	usta	zub
Finnish....	üksi	kaksi	kolme	päː	silmä	korvɑ	nenä	suː	hammas
Estonian..	üks	kaks	kolm	pea	silm	wilja-pea	nina	suː	hammas
Hungarian......	ed	keːt	haːrom	föː, fej	sem	fül	orr	saːj	fog
Basque ...	bat	bi	hirür	bürü	begi	belari	südür	aho	orts

possible: (1) into one family in one way /ABCD/; (2) into two families, seven ways, /ABC/D/, /ABD/C/, /ACD/B/, /BCD/A/, /AB/CD/, /AC/BD/, /AD/BC/; (3) into three families, six ways, /AB/C/D/, /AC/B/D/, /AD/B/C/, /CD/A/B/, /BD/A/C/, /BC/A/D/; (4) into four families, one way, /A/B/C/D/. This makes

---

3. The mass comparison of basic vocabulary is actually the oldest method employed. Essentially correct results were obtained in the eighteenth century even from very poor descriptive material. The earliest instance of which I am aware is Philip John von Strahlenberg, *An Historic-geographic description of the Northern and Eastern Parts of Europe and Asia* (English translation [London, 1738] from German original edition of 1730).

a total of fourteen ways. With the increasing number of languages, the number of distinct ways of classifying increases at a tremendous rate. For eight languages the number is already 4,140.[4] For twenty-five, the number of languages in Table 3, the possible ways of classifying are 4,749,027,089,305,918,018, that is, nearly 5 quintillion or 5×10^{18}. Otherwise put, the method of vocabulary comparison, after the examination of two words, has already selected out of nearly 5 quintillion possibilities exactly that one which is, by universal consent and much other evidence, accepted as the correct one! There must be good reasons for this result. It has been the purpose of this chapter to explain what they are.

The correct hypothesis may not appear quite so quickly in every case, but even supposedly distant relationships, e.g., Algonkian-Ritwan, Austroasiatic, appear fairly soon and are confirmed again and again.

The methods outlined here do not conflict in any fashion with the traditional comparative method. They may be viewed rather as an attempt to make explicit the first step in that method itself, for we cannot begin systematic reconstruction until we know which languages to compare. The application of the comparative method is a continuous process, and, in principle, there is no sharp break between its initial and its more advanced stages. Thus at the very beginning, under the guise of the apparently synchronic concept of sound resemblance, what is being considered by the experienced observer is the diachronic probability that the compared sounds are independent continuations of the same original sound. This, on the whole, coincides with synchronic similarity on an articulatory basis, since sound changes normally involve the change of a single feature of articulation at a time. Such judgments are further guided by our accumulation of knowledge of attested sound changes in other language groups.

Indeed, the very act of noting form-meaning resemblances involves notions of correspondence and reconstruction. If we compare English 'hænd and German 'hant, we do so on the assumption that the h in both forms corresponds, that English æ corresponds to German a, etc., and not to h or to n. Moreover, however incompletely, reconstruction of an original sound system is involved. If I equate English æ and German a, this is on the assumption of a common origin; and the original form, while not precisely determined, is strongly limited to those sounds which could have given rise to both æ and a. It was very probably some low, unrounded vowel like a, far less likely i, and certainly not k. Moreover, the procedure of mass comparison advocated here helps to make the conjecture regarding the ancestral sound ever more precise by the addition of further forms from additional languages. The test provided by the tendency to converge backward in time as each form is compared

---

4. The number of possible classifications for $n + 1$ languages is obtained recursively from that of n languages by the formula:

$$p_{n+1} = \sum_{i=0}^{n} \binom{n}{i} p_i \, ;$$

cf. Oystein Ore, "Theory of Equivalence Relations," *Duke Mathematics Journal*, 1942, pp. 573–627.

within its own subgroup of the larger family which was earlier stated as an integral part of the method determining genetic relationship involves this type of preliminary reconstruction.

The further application of the comparative method resulting in more precise reconstruction is built on a systematic utilization of the etymologies disclosed by preliminary comparison. These etymologies are of varying strength, depending on the following factors: phonetic resemblance, semantic plausibility, breadth of distribution in the various subgroups of the family, length, participation in parallel irregular alternations, and the occurrence of sound correspondences found in other etymologies which are strong on these same grounds. More advanced reconstruction will add some new etymologies and/or invalidate some of the weaker original ones. Those etymologies that are strong on the basis of the criteria mentioned cannot, I believe, be invalidated by the later reconstructions of the sound system. It is rather the efficiency of such reconstructions in explaining these etymologies that is the touchstone by which such reconstructions are tested. Unless etymologies of this degree of strength existed, we would not have been justified in drawing a conclusion of genetic relationship in the first place.

This is clear from actual practice. The Latin form *quattuor*, "four," is a first-rate etymology because it is long, exhibits recurrent correspondences in most of its parts, occurs in every branch of Indo-European, and is semantically straightforward. However, the double *t* remains unexplained. The Indo-Europeanist does not therefore reject *quattuor* as a valid etymology. He seeks rather to explain it by other recognized historical processes, such as the analogical influence of other numerals. In other words, reconstruction of an original sound system has the status of an explanatory theory to account for etymologies already strong on other grounds. Between the **vaida* of Bopp and the **γwoidxe* of Sturtevant lie more than a hundred years of the intensive development of Indo-European phonological reconstruction. What has remained constant has been the validity of the etymologic relationship among Sanskrit *veda*, Greek *woida*, Gothic *wait*, all meaning "I know," and many other unshakable etymologies both of root and of non-root morphemes recognized at the outset. And who will be bold enough to conjecture from what original the Indo-Europeanist one hundred years from now will derive these same forms? Thus reconstruction is in itself a continuous process, although the human effort may be discontinuous and pause after the first stages through lack of refined descriptive data or qualified and interested specialists; and this process goes onward indefinitely into the unknown future.

CHAPTER IV

THE PROBLEM OF LINGUISTIC SUBGROUPINGS

BOTH German and archaic English have in common an -st suffix indicating the second person singular of the verb: German *du denk-st;* English *thou think-est.* Given the relatively close genetic relationship of English and German, the obvious explanation is one of common origin, that is, that both forms are the continuations of a Proto-Germanic -st, second person-singular suffix in both English and German. The known history of these forms, however, shows something quite different. Both German and English inherited a second person singular in -s. In both languages, independently, the suffixation of the independent pronoun in question led to a form in -st, which then spread by analogy to non-interrogative constructions: *þinkes-þu, þinkest; denkes-du, denkest.*[1] The forms are thus the results neither of common origin from an original *-st nor of borrowing; they are convergent developments. Yet convergence in this instance cannot mean accident. Had not both languages possessed an inherited second person in -s, a second person singular independent pronoun beginning with a dental, and an interrogative construction involving inversion, the common end result could not have occurred. A common stage had been set. Small wonder, then, that a similar act ensued. We have, then, a specific resemblance in form and meaning which is a complex resultant of genetic relationship and convergence. Similar instances can be found in non-linguistic cultural history. Oriental scholars have long been struck by the general similarities of Egyptian and Sumerian cultures, accompanied by only minor instances of resemblances that can have resulted from direct historic contact. In this sense Egyptian and Sumerian cultures are not historically related. Yet it is surely no accident that in the same general area of the world and in the same chronologic period, cities, priesthoods, and a host of other important similar cultural features developed. Here again, on a genetically related base in neolithic culture, like developments occurred independently. This process in language is what Sapir called "drift"; it may quite simply be defined as convergence among genetically related languages.

Other complex causes of sound-meaning resemblances may be suggested. Bloomfield once cited as an example of the hazards of linguistic reconstruction the possibility of constructing a Proto-Central-Algonkian word for "whiskey." These lan-

---

1. Perhaps other factors entered into the history of the forms. Both in English and in German there were two preterite presents with inherited -st from earlier *-t-t in the second person singular, which could have provided an analogic￼l model. These are OE *wāst,* Modern German *weisst,* "thou knowest," and Modern English *must,* German *musst.* In this case, the basis for convergence is even wider.

guages, all starting from cognate words for *fire* and cognate words for *water* and in possession of a common Algonkian pattern of compounding, produced words similar in form and meaning which are not the result of common inheritance. This instance differs somewhat from the previous Germanic example, in that the developments were not independent. The semantic pattern of compounding a word *fire-water* for "whiskey" presumably spread through borrowing of meaning pattern only (semantic borrowing) over a large area of Amerindian languages, including both Algonkian and non-Algonkian languages. Only in the Algonkian languages, however, did they produce sound-meaning resemblances because of the existence of a common genetic basis. The Algonkian forms for "whiskey" result, then, from a complex of common inheritance and semantic borrowing.

In Portuguese, as spoken in the United States, the term *livraria*, from meaning "bookshop" as it does in European Portuguese, has taken on the meaning "library" because of its resemblance in sound to the English word. This is again a resemblance in both sound and meaning. Although Portuguese and English are ultimately related, the existence of "library" in English is, of course, the result of borrowing from Romance languages. The specific shift in American Portuguese stems from English semantic influence, not direct borrowing. This illustrates still another complex cause of sound-meaning likeness—ordinary borrowing combined with semantic borrowing.

These examples are cited because of their relevance to the problem of subclassification of languages. Did we not know the history of -*st* through written records, this resemblance between English and German, not shared by other Germanic languages, might well be taken as evidence in favor of a common origin of English and German distinct from that of other Germanic languages. That is, we would consider this form as pointing toward a special grouping within Germanic which opposed English and German as descended from a distinct intermediate speech community to one or more other such intermediate communities as ancestors of the other Germanic languages. From this example, it is apparent that convergence among related languages is a different and more subtle problem than simple convergence among unrelated languages. Given the same starting point, we may expect that similar quite specific results may ensue without historic contact. As in the establishment of genetic relationship, it is sound-meaning resemblances that count; but the entire weighting is different, which is what lends the problem its methodological interest. To cite another instance, if two languages have the form *mata*, "eye," this is evidence which weighs positively in establishing genetic relationship. If, however, two different Malayo-Polynesian languages both have *mata*, "eye," this same fact is of practically no moment as an indication of a special relationship between the two languages within Malayo-Polynesian. Here the well-nigh universal distribution of *mata* prevents it from functioning as evidence for any one particular form of subgrouping, while it is precisely this universal distribution which is a cogent indication of the common origin of the family as a whole.

The problem of genetic subgrouping is thus one which is methodologically distinct, though related, to that of the establishment of genetic relationship. It has given rise to far less general discussion. Subgroupings are often done in a casual manner, and differences of opinion in their regard are generally considered of relatively minor significance. Yet the specific historical relationship implied, being more recent in time, may be of far greater interest to the ethnologist and culture historian. The establishment of a large linguistic stock either with incorrect subgrouping or with no subgrouping at all can lead to serious errors of historical interpretation. Such a family as Hokan-Siouan, covering as it does large portions of North and Central America, can lead to a vast variety of conflicting interpretations unless accompanied by detailed and accurate subgrouping. The problem is thus in its way quite as important as the more frequently discussed one of genetic relationship, and it is often far more difficult of solution.

The relative ease or difficulty of the subgrouping problem rests ultimately on the ratios of several time spans. We now no longer ask whether A, B, and C are related.

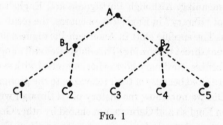

Fig. 1

We ask the more subtle question, given the relationship of A, B, and C, is the distance between A and B equal to, or less than, the distance from A to C? If less, then AB groups as distinct from C. Our explanation is that the speech community ancestral to all three at one time split into a number of language communities, from one of which A and B have descended by further differentiation and from another of which C has arisen.

There are, then, three points of time to consider, or more, if further and finer subgrouping can be carried out. Methodologically, it will be simpler to consider the minimum case of three time points.

Figure 1 indicates that five contemporary related languages—C_1, C_2, C_3, C_4, and C_5—group into two branches, one consisting of C_1 and C_2, the other of C_3, C_4, and C_5. Language B_1 is ancestral to C_1 and C_2; B_2 to C_3, C_4, and C_5, while A is ancestral to the entire group. The three points of time are A, B, and C; the two intervals of time A–B and B–C. The comparative length of these two periods A–B and B–C has important consequences. If the earlier period A–B is very long compared to the subsequent period B–C, that is, if the ratio A–B/B–C is large, the problem is easy of solution. During the relatively long period A–B, many independent changes have occurred in the two branches, with little change in the ensuing period B–C to obliterate the results. In this situation, recognition of relationship among the languages of each branch often precedes that of the existence of the family as a whole. For example, the relationship among the Semitic languages was noted long before that of the larger Afro-Asiatic (Hamito-Semitic) family, which contains Semitic as a branch. We may presume that the groups of languages which at an earlier stage were recognized as independent families are valid branches of the larger family, since the differences among the branches are here so great that each was recognized as a separate entity before the family as a whole came to be accepted. However, grouping errors may arise even here, and the whole problem should be re-examined after the establishment of the larger family.

The opposite extreme is found where the ratio A–B/B–C is small. The earlier period here is short, with the consequent opportunity for only a small number of changes, while the subsequent period is long, allowing for the obliteration of these changes. These are the difficult cases in which, as with the Bantu or Malayo-Polynesian languages, relationship of the languages to one another as a whole was early recognized but where even at present there is no satisfactory subgrouping.

The problem of subgrouping, then, is the recognition of the existence of a set of changes common to a particular subgroup which has occurred between the period of divergences of the family as a whole and that of the subgroup in question (the time periods A–B_1 and A–B_2 of Fig. 1). It is a dynamic problem of the detection of changes. Even when phrased as though it employed criteria based on the synchronic sharing of features, a historical analysis is implied. Thus, if reference is made to an item of vocabulary found in certain related languages but not in others, this static phraseology conceals the fact that it is the process of replacement of one item of vocabulary by another which is decisive. As has long been seen, the essential factor is shared innovations, since shared retentions can always occur independently without a common period of development. Shared obsolescences can be of some significance when connected with a functional replacement. If two languages replace an earlier word for "nose" with some other term and also lose the traditional term, this double agreement is of significance for judging the existence of a common historical period.

The detection of such common innovations and obsolescences encounters special difficulties; since the languages all have a common starting point, the chance of convergence—the process of drift mentioned in the earlier part of this chapter—is very great. The problem of borrowing is also multiplied, in that closely allied languages are certainly more likely to borrow even fundamental vocabulary and grammatical affixes than more distant forms of speech. In dealing with the task of subgrouping, we have not four but five causes of sound-meaning resemblances to take into account: chance, symbolism, borrowing, genetic inheritance from the common period of the entire family, and genetic inheritance from the period of common development of the language ancestral to the subbranch. In distinguishing these last two, a typical danger of circular reasoning must be surmounted. Since occurrence in at least two separate branches of a family is the common reason for assigning a feature to the ancestral language of the family as a whole, a resemblance between two languages can be assigned to this early period if the two languages are classified in separate branches. In this case the feature is judged to be a retention and not indicative of a special relation between the two languages. On the other hand, we can consider the resemblance as evidence that the two languages belong to the same branch of the family. In this case the feature is judged to be a common innovation and not to be part of the protolanguage of the family as a whole.

One solution to this problem is the bringing to bear of evidence from languages more distantly related to the family as a whole, where such exist. The entire problem then remains, in a sense, one of subgrouping, but on a wider scale. For example, in Bantu languages, a few terms for parts of the human body, "ear," "arm," and "armpit," are found commonly with the prefix *ku-* and just as commonly with *li-*. Proto-Bantu is generally reconstructed as having the *li-* prefix for the words "ear," "arm," and "armpit." The argument for *ku-* is, I believe, much stronger. An analogical change from *ku-* to *li-* is easily understandable, since *ku-* is not otherwise used with ordinary nouns, being typically an infinitive and locative prefix, whereas *li-* is very common and includes many other terms for parts of the human body. The motive for a change from *li-* to *ku-* is hard to discover. Moreover, a few languages have *liku-*, but none have *kuli-*. Here the *ku-* was not understood as a prefix, and *li-* was then prefixed to the whole form analogically. Aside from any judgment of the internal Bantu evidence, however, this question is decided in favor of *ku-* by its frequent appearance in the most widely scattered branches of the vast Niger-Congo family of which Bantu is but a subbranch, contrasted with the non-occurrence of *li-* outside Bantu. Again, there are variant Bantu forms for "two," *bali* and *bili*, both about equally widespread. We might make a rather uncertain choice in favor of *bali* as earlier, on the assumption that *bali* > *bili* might occur as a sporadic instance of vowel harmony. In fact, the evidence from other Niger-Congo languages is again decisive and in favor of *bali*. The form *bili* is never found anywhere outside Bantu. This, incidentally, allows us to judge *bili* as an innovation, the sharing of which is evidence of the existence of a separate subbranch within Bantu, while the occurrence of *bali*, a retention, has no such implications. These and many other examples which could be cited are of interest because they refute the common belief that more remote relationships should be ignored, while each distinct subbranch is reconstructed separately and independently. In many cases we cannot choose between alternative reconstructions without taking the wider family into account. In fact, in Indo-European the reconstruction of the protolanguage of the family as a whole progressed far more rapidly than did that of the individual branches. Moreover, Proto-Germanic and other comparable intermediate unities have always been reconstructed with one eye backward to Proto-Indo-European and one eye forward to the contemporary Germanic languages.

Let us now consider some of the types of linguistic change with a view to their value in determining subgroupings. Starting with phonology, regular sound changes can be seen to be generally of little value in this regard. The possible number of changes is small, and the probability of convergences high. Thus in Indo-European the voiced aspirates have, without doubt, become unaspirated stops a number of times independently. A conditioned change, i.e., one in which one phoneme has changed to another only under certain stated conditions, is of somewhat greater value, but any single one of these also easily results from convergent developments.

The sharing of a whole series of changes is of greater cogency. For example, the Malayo-Polynesian languages seem to fall into two main subgroups, a western and an eastern. Among other features, the sharing of a whole series of phoneme mergers by the eastern languages is certainly an important item of evidence. Certain western languages, for example, Malagasy, have independently carried out some of the changes, but not all of them.

What appears at first glance as an impressive series of shared phonemic changes may, on closer inspection, turn out not to be at all decisive. A good many of the changes stated by Grimm in his first law, referring to the transition from Proto-Indo-European to Proto-Germanic, also occur independently in Armenian. But the whole series of changes resolves itself into a few interconnected habit changes which have also occurred in other non-related languages. The changes $b > p$, $d > t$, and $g > k$ are all the consequences of a single change in the habit of articulation from voiced to unvoiced sounds. The changes $p > f$, $t > \not{p}$, and $k > x$, which are also included in the statement of Grimm's law, likewise involve a single change of habit from stop to fricative articulation. Moreover, as Martinet has pointed out, such changes are interconnected as the result of a general tendency to greater or lesser vigor of articulation at certain historic periods. Indeed, this whole set of changes recurs in Angas of the Chad branch of the Afroasiatic languages and elsewhere.

Sporadic changes, such as individual assimilations and dissimilations, are of greater moment, in that they are less likely to happen independently. However, such common tendencies as the dissimilation of one of two l sounds to an r can certainly occur convergently. Still, the number of possibilities is greater here, since each is an independent case. The sporadic changes $n > r$ in Aramaic *bar*, "son," and $l > r$ in *tarten*, "three" (cf. Hebrew *ben* and *šɔlɔš*, respectively), are practically certain indications of membership of a dialect in the Aramaic rather than the Canaanite branch of Northwest Semitic. To sum up, unconditioned changes, if large in number, shared conditioned changes, and sporadic sound changes are all evidence of subgrouping. A single unconditioned change is of practically no value at all.

In the area of morphological change, the most important single process is analogy. In general, shared analogies are of little help for the problem under consideration, since the pressure of more frequent on less frequent patterns is everywhere great and likely to lead to similar changes. On the other hand, sharing of a highly irregular alternation, which, as we have seen, is of great weight indeed as an indication of genetic relationship, is useless in the present instance. A highly irregular formation which has withstood analogy must be very old. It is a common retention, not an innovation, and therefore irrelevant for such grouping. Thus we arrive at the somewhat discouraging conclusion that both analogical change, if it follows the dominant pattern, and absence of analogical change are equally indecisive as indications of subgroupings. An illustrative example is furnished by the common Indo-European demonstrative and third person pronoun. In the nominative singular masculine, some languages have reflexes of an original *so (e.g., Greek *ho,* "the"); other languages of an original *sos (e.g., Sanskrit *sas*). The masculine singular nominative without the usual *-s* is an anomaly. There is no analogical pattern that could lead to the loss of *-s* independently in a number of instances, whence Indo-Europeanists unanimously reconstruct *so as Proto-Indo-European. The agreement of two languages in retaining reflexes of *so is therefore merely a common retention and no evidence for a separate group. On the other hand, the pattern of a nominative masculine singular in *-s* is predominant in other forms, so that the addition of *-s* is a natural analogic development which can easily occur in separate instances.

The following example of a rare analogical pattern is much less likely to be the result of convergence. The perfect *y-t-n,* "give," shared by Phoenician and Ugaritic is a quite strong argument for the affiliation of Ugaritic with the Canaanite branch of Semitic to which Phoenician belongs. Elsewhere in Semitic the perfect is *n-t-n.* It was probably the possession of a common imperative and imperfect formation without initial consonant in both verbs with initial *n* and *y* that provided the model: *šb:tn* (imperatives) = *yšb:ytn* (perfect). Since both initial *n-* and initial *y-* verbs are uncommon and since the shift of membership has occurred only in this single verb and in the same direction—from the *n-* to the *y-* class—in both Ugaritic and Canaanite, it is highly unlikely to have occurred independently in the two cases. In view of the geographical proximity of the two languages, borrowing as an alternative explanation is much more likely than convergence if this irregularity is to be rejected as evidence of the Canaanite affiliation of Ugaritic.

A morphological construction, for example, <u>a periphrasis of verb root and auxiliary to</u> form a tense involving the existing elements not hitherto combined or, better still, at least one element which is uncommon elsewhere in the family, <u>is powerful evidence for subgrouping.</u> The common possession of a future in *-b* by Italic and Celtic languages is a case in point. Such a combination is unlikely to have occurred independently, although even this is not impossible; one of the common theories derives this formation from a periphrasis with *bhu,* "to become." The existence of another, more common future in *-s* elsewhere in Indo-European suggests that the *-b* future is an innovation. In other words, where a replacement has occurred not involving some common analogical formation, the possibility of convergence becomes small. That is, this would be so, were we sure that there was functional replacement. Proto-Indo-European might have had two futures with different semantic functions of which only one survived in any given language. The danger of circular reasoning again rears its head. The appearance of *-b* in Italic and Celtic can be evaluated as evidence that the formation is Proto-Indo-European if an Italo-Celtic branch is not accepted.

Lexical innovations are of great value because convergence is practically ruled out. That, for example, two Indo-European languages would independently make up a new verb "to take" with the form *nem is extremely unlikely. Though convergence is thus virtually ruled out, borrowing becomes an important alternative explanation, since it is among lexical items that dialect borrowing is most frequent. In detecting lexical innovations, the existence of as complete materials as possible for each language concerned becomes of major importance. If the material is very limited, it may appear that a particular group of languages shared a common term not found elsewhere. Fuller evidence may disclose the existence of a cognate with slightly different meaning in some other language in the family. What appears to be a lexical innovation thus becomes merely a semantic shift in at least one language or group of languages. While this is also evidence, it is far less convincing than a complete lexical innovation.

This brings us to the topic of semantic change. It is obvious that meaning changes are strongly subject to convergence. Moreover, it is often difficult to know what is retention and what is innovation, for a semantic shift which takes place in one direction can often just as easily occur in reverse fashion. A term for "day" often becomes "sun," but likewise a term that means "sun" frequently comes to mean "day."

From this review of some of the more common types of linguistic changes, it will be seen that there is hardly a feature shared by certain related languages and not others for which convergence or borrowing is absolutely excluded as an explanation. Nevertheless, when in even more difficult cases the evidence is examined closely and in the light of general comparative reconstruction of the linguistic history of the entire family, certain groupings will normally emerge. Although, as has been noted, no single resemblance is ever completely decisive, it will be found that certain languages share with one another a far larger number of features which may be innovations than they do with related languages outside the subgroup and that among these are some of those which are least likely to be the result of convergence, including shared sound shifts en masse, sporadic sound changes, new morphological formations, shared analogical shifts, including some of the rarer ones, and true lexical innovations. It is the sheer number of such resemblances, together with the inclusion of some of the types most likely to be innovations, that excludes convergence or borrowing as an over-all explanation.

The present chapter outlines the type of evidence to be considered in arriving at subgroupings. It by no means follows that such evidence will always be found. The reason may be that, while such subgroupings do exist, the period of common development of each subgroup is short and its period of subsequent differentiation long, as has been noted. In difficult cases, such as this, the lack of sufficient first-rate descriptive grammatical and lexical material for the languages and of adequate linguistic reconstruction prevents us from assembling and judging adequately the evidence for the groupings which are actually present. In other cases no grouping may exist. There is no a priori reason for denying this. If linguistic innovations in a speech community spread in a random way, such as that envisaged by the classical wave theory, then there would be gradual transitions only and no sharp breaks anywhere to give rise to distinct groupings. Wherever migrations or the intrusions of peoples speaking non-related languages occur, innovations encounter a barrier which cannot regularly be overcome, and sharp groupings inevitably result. This has often occurred, e.g., the separation of Rumanian from the rest of the Romance speech community. With or without actual movements of people of this sort, language families often display clear divisions into branches. The pure wave model therefore cannot be universally correct. Although, as has been seen, absence of sub-grouping is a possibility, it seems more likely that the non-linguistic forces which produce differentiation into separate tribes, political states, and economic regions must have a profound effect on spoken communication, producing weakness in lines of communication which gives rise to dialects and eventually separate languages and language subgroups as the process continues.

The problem of discovering subgroupings is, in the more difficult cases, quite arduous, far more so than the discovery of genetic relationships. The principles discussed here are not essentially new. They may be found, for example, in the classic treatment of Brugmann.[2] I do not believe that there are any short cuts. Recently glottochronological methods[3] have been used. No doubt in less difficult cases this will lead to accurate results. However, the mere counting of the number of cognates shared, without attention to morphological or phonologic evidence and without consideration of the general distribution of each form for its bearing on the question of innovation, is a relatively crude method which disregards much relevant evidence. If, for example, we were using the method of glottochronology to group the Indo-European languages, under the number "four" we would have, among other entries, English *four*, German *vier*, Danish *fir*, Italian *quattro*, Spanish *cuatro*, French *quatre*. Since these are all cognate, we would simply score this as a single agreement among all the languages concerned, and it would contribute no information toward the problem of subgrouping. Yet English, German, and Danish here share innovations in the form of the word, loss of *t*, *qu* > *f*, etc., which Italian, Spanish, and French do not. Hence valuable relevant features are being overlooked.

This criticism of the adequacy of glottochronological methods for this problem is not meant to detract from its possible value as an approximate quantitative measure of the periods of time involved, once the subgrouping problem has been solved by conventional methods.

In cases of obvious subgrouping, the correct results will be very quickly evident from comparative vocabulary inspection, as described in the previous chapter on genetic relationship. This method will show lexical innovations, as well as some new morphological combinations, widespread sound changes, and sporadic shifts. In

2. Karl Brugmann, "Zur Frage nach den Verwandschaftsverhältnissen der idg. Sprachen," *Internationale Zeitschrift für allgemeine Sprachwissenschaft*, I (1883), 225–56.

3. See, for example, Samuel H. Elbert, "Internal Relationships of Polynesian Lagnuages and Dialects," *Southwestern Journal of Anthropology*, IX (1953), 147–73.

more difficult cases, vocabulary inspection should also furnish an answer, but only after meticulous examination of the distribution of each form and of the relevant phonological and semantic factors. However, the examination of morphology, if the languages have a complex morphological system, and considerations from the development of the sound system of each language based on reconstruction will in such cases often lead to more rapid results. In so far as the data and state of historical knowledge allow, all types of evidence should be considered. The results in all these domains will necessarily agree if the evidence examined is relevant and due weight is accorded each item.

CHAPTER V

LANGUAGE AND EVOLUTIONARY THEORY

I N THE present and the subsequent two chapters, only one of the many ways in which the science of language is related to other sciences dealing with cultural behavior will be systematically considered. The group of problems selected may be described as the interpretation and evaluation of various theories of culture in the light of the data provided by language. This particular facet of what may be broadly termed "ethnolinguistics" has apparently been little considered up to now. It is a generally accepted thesis that language is a part of the cultural behavior of peoples. Linguistics is thus logically a branch of cultural anthropology, the general science which is concerned with such behavior. However, linguistics has existed in addition to this affiliation and continues to flourish outside anthropology in the general academic division of labor and is the heir of concepts and theories independently derived and often antedating those of anthropology as a whole. The inevitable result of such historically conditioned disparity is that the application of cultural theories, usually conceived without any, or with only minor, reference to language, requires as a preliminary the interpretation of such terminology into the traditional frame of reference employed in linguistics. This in itself has an intrinsic value as a step toward the unification of terminology within anthropology. More important, it allows us to employ linguistic data as a test of theories of culture. One putative advantage to be gained from the analysis of language often adduced by anthropologists is its transparency. But granting the truth of this observation, the transparency of the data will be of no avail if the terminology in which it is traditionally described is such as to mask its relevance for cultural theory. The present essays do not claim to be more than a modest beginning of this complex and frequently difficult task.

The concept of evolution is one of wide significance, as is evident from its central role in certain philosophical systems and from the breadth of its applications in a variety of disciplines ranging from the natural and biological sciences (cosmic, terrestrial, and animal evolution) to the social sciences and humanities, particularly cultural anthropology and history. A concept of such far-flung uses necessarily differs much in individual instances, so much so that at times it seems difficult to discover the common elements underlying the diversity of applications. Several prevalent uses of the term "evolution" may be eliminated at the outset as inappropriate. One instance is the use of the term to mean orderly change in general. In this sense the existence of evolutionary phenomena is simply an affirmation of the basic scientific faith that the universe is ordered and coherent and therefore susceptible to the explanatory methods of science. If this is what is indicated by "evolution," no scientist, at least, is likely to disagree. It is evident, however, that something at once more distinctive and more controversial is usually indicated by the term.

Another meaning, which may be rejected, on the contrary ground of overspecificity, is that of "gradual" as opposed to "revolutionary" or sudden change. This usage is pretty much confined to sociology and political science. In these realms the existence of both types of social change is admitted as a fact. By some stretching of terminology, perhaps the term "revolutionary" might also be extended to the catastrophic changes in geology assumed by the advocates of the early Neptunian and Vulcanian theories. The concept of gradual, as opposed to violent, change seems too narrow to constitute the basis of a general concept of evolution. Still, both coherence and gradualness do play a certain role in the more generally applicable formulations of evolutionary theory to be outlined here.

Perhaps we may come closer to the essential ideas underlying all evolutionary approaches by considering that in every case we have to do with the explanation of how a variety of forms, whether biological species, languages, or cultural systems, came to be. Two general types of explanation exist which we may call the "creationist" and the "transformist." The former, with sporadic exceptions, held the field until the turn of the nineteenth century. In its purest version it assumes that all kinds are unchangeable, except for more or less haphazard modifications within the bounds of the type, and have existed in their present form since they came into being by a single act of creation. Such was the generally accepted view regarding biological species before Darwin, and such likewise was the traditional Tower of Babel explanation of the origin of language diversity.

The opposite view is that all existing forms are historically connected by a dynamic process of growth. On this view, the greater the similarity among existing forms, the more recent the common ancestry. But, whether less remotely or more remotely, all forms are ultimately connected by descent. As a further consequence, common ancestors are forms different from any existing today and are conceived to be such as to give rise to present forms by differential independent development. Such growth is viewed as, in general, gradual and coherent, allowing for minor leaps, such as those induced by mutations in biology. Were changes sudden and capricious, anything might issue from anything at a not too distant remove, and the observed natural groupings of species would not occur. The employment of the term "evolution" exclusively for gradual change or coherence in change mentioned earlier is implied by these considerations.

In fact, creationism and transformism in their pure forms are polar concepts between which gradations are possible. On an extreme transformist view, all forms are related by ultimate common origin. There must therefore be some single primeval form from which all others developed. Monogenesis is therefore logically required. It would be possible to maintain a more moderate transformism in which each existing form is connected with at least some others but not with all, as a consequence of several distinct creations. Biologists who postulate connecting forms among some of the phyla for which plausible common ancestry cannot at present be found are espousing the monogenist version of transformism. It is clearly possible to assume, with polygenists, several creations where links cannot be found and still deny that species are fixed types. Another intermediate view is that adopted by most geologists for a time in the nineteenth century to account for fossils. The belief was rejected that existing species are the unchanged continuations of the species created at the beginning while the fixity of species was maintained. From time to time all species were supposed to have been destroyed and new ones created without affiliation by descent from the forms of the previous era. In this fashion the basic notion of fixity of kinds could be maintained. This approach may be termed "catastrophism." There are thus four basic types of explanation of specific diversity: the evolutionary monogenetic, the evolutionary polygenetic, the creationist, and the catastrophic. The first and third assume single creations, the second and fourth, multiple creations; the first and second, transformation of species, the third and fourth, fixity of species.

In the sense of transformism, whether monogenetic or polygenetic, evolution was an accepted theory in linguistics earlier than in biology, though not under that name. The recognition that the resemblance of certain languages to one another is to be explained by common descent is the fundamental hypothesis underlying the concept of genetic relationship among languages. In Semitic studies for one, such theories were already held in the eighteenth century. The recognition of the Indo-European family at the turn of the nineteenth century is the single event which marks most clearly the birth of modern linguistic science. The evidence at that time led, as it still leads, to a polygenetic theory, since not all languages can be demonstrated to have a common origin. But, as in biology, the assumption of a similar process of differentiation for an earlier period and the absence of any proof of spontaneous generation in historic times lend plausibility to the speculation of monogenesis. Some day the problem may well be solved by the indirect evidence of anthropology, psychology, and general linguistic science.

The essential likeness between genetic theories in language and the evolutionary hypothesis in biology was explicitly recognized by Schleicher, a leading linguist of the nineteenth century. In his work *Die Darwinsche Theorie und die Sprachwissenschaft*, he treats evolutionary theory in biology as, in principle, the equivalent of the genetic model of linguistic relationship.[1] In this, the transformationist sense, then, language may be said to evolve, and the recognition of the fact in linguistic science preceded its general acceptance in biology.

But a further idea seems to be required by the term "evolution" in its most generally accepted sense. A theory, for example, which regarded all species as interconnected but which posited some mammalian form as the primeval ancestral type, whence descended in one line all the other vertebrates, in another the ancestor of all non-vertebrate phyla, with Protozoa first appearing in a very recent period, would

1. August Schleicher, *Die Darwinsche Theorie und die Sprachwissenschaft* (Berlin, 1863); see also the discussion in Hermann Paul, *Prinzipien der Sprachgeschichte* (Halle, 1909).

not be adjudged a representative evolutionary theory. In addition to the notion of transformation, another—that of progress or advance of some kind—is evidently required. Before examining further this idea of progress, its logical distinctness from transformism should be noted. For example, a holder of the catastrophic theory may well believe that each successive creation represents progress over previous ones. In fact, geologists in general accepted progress while denying transformation of species for a considerable period during the nineteenth century. It is well at the outset also to distinguish the fact of evolutionary advance, if it should turn out to be possible to characterize it in some objective fashion, from the ethical judgment that this advance is good which often accompanies it and tends to be the motivation for accepting its validity. The judgment that evolutionary advance exists and is good I shall call "progress." The fact itself I shall call "advance" or "evolutionary advance." The belief in evolutionary advance is compounded of the belief in some scale on which species or kinds can be rated as more or less advanced and the belief that, on the whole, less advanced forms have preceded more advanced forms in time.

In what way, for example, can man be said to be more advanced than an amoeba (N.B., not better)? The classic definition of Spencer states this difference in terms of heterogeneity and complexity as characteristic of advanced forms. But it is not heterogeneity or complexity as such which constitutes advance on the usual view. For example, the simplification of the toes of the horse to form the hoof, which resulted in more efficient running, would be considered evolutionary advance. The single comprehensive law of Newton is an advance over Kepler's three laws of motion. In general, in the words of Herrick, it is "change in the direction of and increase in the range and variety of adjustments to environment" which is involved.[2] Among developments that may be considered as advance, there are, on the perceptual side, ability to respond to finer discriminations of stimuli, to stimuli from a greater distance, and to new ranges of stimuli, e.g., a new sense. On the motor or effector side the ability to live in a greater range of temperature, moisture, or other physical conditions of environment, speed of movement, and the ability to make finer manipulatory adjustments of objects in the environment may be cited as examples. In the intervening activity between perception and response comes the co-ordination of responses and the lesser or greater appropriateness of responses to stimuli, e.g., the development of a central nervous system, of social co-operation, and of intelligence in general.

This gives us many facets of comparison. Most, or perhaps even all, are, in principle, subject to objective comparative, even quantitative, evaluation. For example, we can measure speed of muscular response by reaction time, speed of locomotion in feet per minute, etc. Still, judgments on these varied scales may well show that, of two species, one is more advanced in some respect, one in another. This is what leads some biologists to say that each species is a perfect adaptation in its own way. Yet undoubtedly, on an over-all basis, man is more advanced than the amoeba; many similar judgments can be made. Moreover, it is a reasonable expectation,

2. *Science*, 1946, p. 469.

borne out by the paleontological record, that, *on the whole*, less advanced have preceded more advanced species. This might well be expected, for fineness of perceptual discrimination, the development of new organs of sense, the genesis and expansion of a central nervous system, the differentiation of specialized motor organs, all require time. Some correlation with the afore-mentioned criteria of Spencer—heterogeneity and complexity—may therefore be expected. For enhanced discrimination in perception and response, it can be argued, requires increased specialization of parts and increased complexity of organization of the whole and of each of the constituent organs. Still, complexity is merely an incidental, however frequent, accompaniment of some aspect of efficiency.

If we now turn to language with these considerations in mind, we note that the typical nineteenth-century evolutionary theory of language which established the framework of all subsequent discussion was one which assumed complexity as the sole criterion of evolutionary advance in language, and only one aspect of complexity—morphological complexity—at that. For the nineteenth-century theory, in the standard formulation of Schleicher, set up three stages: isolating, agglutinative, and inflective, each of which was defined basically in terms of the morphological structure of the word. In contemporary terminology an isolating language is one in which each word consists of a single morpheme. In the agglutinative stage words are multimorphemic, but there are, ideally, no irregular morphophonemic alternations. With inflecting languages, there are irregular alternations such that, in principle, the assignment of certain phonemes to one or the other of two morphemes is arbitrary. This is sometimes called "fusion." The line of evolutionary advance, then, is from isolating languages, characterized by the simplest word structure, through the agglutinative to the inflectional stage, marked by the most complex types of formation. This was alternatively characterized as an advance from analytic to synthetic forms of thought or from formless to true form languages.

The ethnocentrism, lack of rigor, and absence of correspondence of these stages with those derivable from non-linguistic culture all led to the general abandonment of the theory. As examples of non-correlation with general cultural evolution, we may note that the isolating, or most primitive, stage had as its most typical representative Chinese; that various American Indian languages turned out to have a more complex word structure than the Indo-European languages; and that in historic times Indo-European languages seemed to be changing from a synthetic to a more analytic or isolating type, a retrograde movement from the viewpoint of the standard theory.

In subsequent discussion it has usually been held that language does not evolve, since there is no correlation between morphological complexity and economic or other criteria of evolutionary advances. This position is assumed even by writers with a predominantly evolutionary approach.[3] A few writers, notably Jespersen, reverse the classical theory. The more primitive a language, the more complex accord-

3. For example, M. Jacobs and B. Stern: "Scientific linguistics has therefore concluded that grammatical complexity appears to correlate little, if at all, with technological or economic levels" (*Outline of Anthropology* [New York, 1947], pp. 283–84).

ing to their view, and evolutionary advances are marked by increasing simplification. Jespersen has, practically alone, considered seriously the problem of efficiency in language.[4] He believes that the greater morphological simplicity of modern European languages, as compared to older forms in the same area, is an advantage and that the general movement of language is in the direction of such simplification. The weakness of Jespersen's treatment is that he has practically confined his interest to Indo-European languages. What is probably an internally conditioned drift toward morphological simplification has therefore been mistaken for a universal linguistic trend. An objective survey fails to disclose any decisive correlation between morphological complexity and the usual criteria of cultural evolution.

From this discussion it is evident that the subject of evolution of language has been treated almost solely in the context of morphological simplicity and complexity. But morphology is only one of the aspects of language. Simplicity in morphology might, for example, be accompanied by great semantic complexity, the presence, as in English, of numerous phrase idioms, of homonyms, and of multiple meanings of the same morpheme (ambiguity). The significance of morphological simplicity or complexity in the over-all picture of language in relation to the work it performs has certainly been overrated. Irregular alternations are, by definition, functionless. The variation between *go* and *wen-* is useless, since the difference in meaning is already expressed by the *-t* of the past. A past *go-ed* would perform the same work and without the burden of learning the alternation, which constitutes a real, if hardly noticed, difficulty for the native speaker and a more conspicuous one for an individual who learns English as a second language. That this is a point of linguistic inefficiency is evidenced by the universal tendency toward analogic change, which typically cancels such functionless alternations. In this matter Jespersen is correct, and the nineteenth-century theorists in error. Morphological simplicity is therefore at least a minor aspect of efficiency, and no discernible advantage accrues to the irregularities which many linguists have tended to glorify. However, as critics of Jespersen have pointed out, while such changes in the direction of morphological efficiency do take place, the process of conditional sound change produces new alternations, so that no over-all movement in the direction of morphological simplicity is discernible.

Recapitulating in the light of our earlier consideration of evolutionary advance, we see that it is not complexity as such that is significant, it is rather the over-all degree of efficiency. But efficiency is meaningful only in terms of some function to be performed. A hoof is more efficient than toes only in relation to speed of locomotion as a function. In the function of manipulation of objects it is less efficient. Hence evolutionary advance can be determined only by reference to function or functions to be performed. The traditional criterion of morphological complexity is here of only minor significance. The basic function of language is communication.[5] This leads us to

4. Among the writings of Jespersen on this topic see particularly *Efficiency in Linguistic Change* (Copenhagen, 1941).

5. By "communication" in this context is meant not only the conveying of information but all those effects on the society and satisfactions of societal needs described as the functions of over-all language activity in the chapter on "Structure and Function in Language" in this work (pp. 75 ff.).

place language in the total frame of the evolution of means of communication. The question of the evolution of language refers to the place of language among other means of communication and whether, in this wider context, a line of evolutionary advance can be discovered. To ask the question regarding language alone is like discussing the evolution of the bow without regard to its position among other weapons.

Means of communication from the standpoint of cosmic evolution can be divided into three stages: prelanguage, language, and postlanguage. Language presumably first appears with hominids. In fact, some would probably want to define hominid in terms of the possession of spoken language. Prelanguage communication is, in the terminology of the first chapter of this work, not a sign system, since there are no combinations of elements subject to grammatical rules. There are signs and even perhaps symbols in the usual acceptation of the terms, but they form no system because there are no constructions involving the combination of elements. Prelanguage signs continue to function even in human societies as gesture and otherwise.

The advantage brought by grammar is chiefly the ability to specify separate aspects of a situation and their relations to one another. Moreover, rules of grammar allow us to combine in constructions aspects not found together in actuality. It becomes possible to state lies, hypotheses, and past and future states of affairs. In the phraseology of semanticists, it is grammar which makes man the time-binding animal.

Natural spoken language is, by general consent, the earliest sign system to appear. In accordance with the normal usage of linguistics, by "language" I shall mean natural spoken language. In addition to the values inherent in any grammatical system, certain advantages of sound as a medium help to explain why language was the first such system to appear. The use of the vocal organs, an overlaid function, did not require the development, through the slow mechanism of genetic change, of a new specialized organ. The voice is always available, involves little physical exertion, and does not interfere with any other activity, except, to a minor degree, eating. Above all, it allows the hands to be free for manipulatory activity. It may be utilized by day as well as night, and it is perceptible in all directions.

Despite all these advantages, language in its physical aspect lacks, above all, permanence and range. Moreover, while the fact that it is not confined to a single channel is, in general, an advantage, under certain circumstances, such as the desire for secrecy or the irrelevance of the message for many within range, separate channels are more useful.

The first advance in the direction of greater physical efficiency is the invention of writing, which gives permanence to speech. The effects of this invention are so great that the difference between civilized and so-called primitive peoples is most frequently defined in terms of it. Recent inventions, such as telegraphy, radio, and teletype, are all designed to give greater range and the possibility of channelized communication.

All these developments have in common that they are isomorphic with language and with one another, at least on the sentence level.[6] Hence any inefficiencies which adhere to the semantic and grammatical systems of language continue unaffected.

In its semantic aspect certain disadvantages of language arise from its method of definition, which is implicit and the result of historic tradition. Dictionaries, which attempt to codify these traditional meanings, exercise a minor influence in the direction of standardization. But the meanings, even when so codified and standardized, commonly suffer from two important defects: ambiguity and vagueness. By "ambiguity" is meant the existence of alternative and different meanings for the same linguistic form, i.e., homonymy. "Vagueness" is the lack of agreement in regard to the instances to be included under a given term. Bertrand Russell gives a striking example. Imagine that speakers of English are confronted with a man without a single hair on his head. Presumably they will agree in the statement that the man in question is bald. Now take a man with a full head of hair and remove the hairs one by one. There will be lack of agreement among speakers of English as to the point at which the statement "the man is bald" is true.

Terms in everyday discourse usually have ambiguous alternative meanings, each of which is, in turn, vague. Ambiguity, in principle, can be eliminated simply by assigning a new and separate term for each ambiguous meaning. Actually, much ambiguity is quite harmless and even a useful conservation of vocabulary resources. For example, the use of the term "case" both in grammatical discourse and in the law courts will presumably mislead no one. Far more insidious than obvious homonyms are the closely similar, but distinct, meanings disclosed only by analysis and tending to persist even in scientific discourse, e.g., the various meanings of "function" in the social and biological sciences and in mathematics.

Vagueness probably cannot be eliminated, for empirical terms at least, but its area can be reduced and its limits specified. For example, we can define a bald man as one who has less than ten active hair follicles. It then remains to define "active hair follicle."

The needs of philosophical and scientific discourse cannot always, in the long run, be satisfied by the use of traditional implicit definition. The first step, which involves a departure from the procedures of traditional language definition, is the use of definition by postulation but within the grammatical and semantic framework of natural language. The physicist defines "force" for his own purposes by explicit agreement, taking as his point of departure its meaning in everyday language, with the understanding that it will have this new meaning in the context of physical discourse.

But sometimes half-measures prove inadequate and, as in the case of mathematics and symbolic logic, an entire sign system is created by postulation or fiat. The form of the symbols, their meaning, and grammatical rules of combination are then all postulated.

6. By this is meant that there are rules of one-to-one transformation between each entire expression of spoken language and some sequence of written or other symbols, without necessary one-to-one correspondence on the element level (as in phonemic writing) or some other level.

A third line of development is the invention of various international languages. These do not, in principle, alter the physical nature of the language sign vehicle. The meanings, though all created by fiat of the inventor, are along traditional language lines and probably are as vague and ambiguous as those of natural language. The one structural advantage of such languages is the practical absence of the dysfunctional morphological complexities of natural languages. Even this advantage accrues almost to the same degree to pidgin languages.

The development of forms isomorphic to language, with the advantages described previously for the physical aspect of communication and the appearance of postulated sign systems which overcome in good part the semantic and grammatical inefficiencies of language, does not mean the supersession of language. It may rather be interpreted as a process of differentiation and specialization within the communication process, whereby each communication need becomes more efficiently served by an instrument which more adequately fulfils some specific function.

In the course of this development language comes more and more to fulfil the functions for which it is most appropriate. The constant availability and flexibility of language suggest that it will not be replaced in person-to-person interaction in the foreseeable future, if ever. Moreover, the abolition of vagueness and ambiguity, whatever its advantages for the purely informational aspects of communication, would result in the probable elimination of humor (certainly of punning, which stems from ambiguity) and of poetry, which flourishes on vagueness. Finally, language plays a unique role in communication, which, aside from all other considerations, doubtless assures its future. If we wish to explain a symbol or a meaning, we do it in a sign system. If the term is still not understood, it must be explained in terms of a sign system of lower level, and so on. But at some point this process must reach an end. Either understanding is achieved, as evidenced by appropriate reaction, or we must resort to the co-ordination of an element or elements of a sign system with that which is not a sign, namely, a set of events. Such a system provides the level of ultimate explanation. Language serves this function, hence its generality as compared with the limited subject matter of other systems or of individual signs. Thus what is sometimes called "art symbolism" is, in a sense, secondary symbolism operating through the symbolism of language. If, for example, I "explain" a Navaho symbolic use of red as referring to the north, I am explaining it in terms of a linguistic symbol "north" which I assume to be understood. So, too, mathematical symbols are ultimately defined in terms of ordinary language.

Ontogenetically, too, we normally learn such symbolisms or postlanguage sign systems after language and in terms of language. Even when, as is possible in the case of gestures, we may learn them before language and independently of language, we may later explain them in terms of language, but never vice versa.

Finally, two other aspects of the evolution of communication may be pointed out which involve the social dimension, that is, the distribution of sign systems with respect to populations. In general, the greater the economic productivity, density of population, and facilities for transportation of persons and goods, the less likely that speech communities will differentiate into many local communities speaking mutually intelligible languages and the more the felt needs of wider communication will result in the development of standard languages and lingua francas, eventuating in extensive monolingual communities. Likewise, the greater differentiation within a group is reflected in specialization within the realm of communication. Before the advent of mass communication, all individuals were of roughly comparable status as senders and receivers of messages, with leadership marked, no doubt, by some degree of superiority in effectiveness, if not of volume of communication. In industrial societies, specialized senders, such as editorial writers, broadcasters, and writers of books, send to far more people than those from whom they receive.

Our general conclusion, then, is that it is not language as such which evolves but rather communication in general. Within this process language does have a central and key position as the source of all postlanguage developments and the general instrument which fulfils the function of the ultimate level of explanation. While it may seem somewhat rash to prejudge the case, it appears that natural languages are all very much on the same level as far as efficiency is concerned. A comparative measure of efficiency which includes all relevant phonological, grammatical, and semantic aspects has never been worked out, and, in view of the complexity of each aspect and the disparity among them, it does not appear very likely that one can be developed. Traditional theories of language evolution have usually taken but one of these aspects, the morphological, and have further assumed a correlation between complexity and advance which is unjustified. Indeed, as we have seen, just the opposite seems more likely to be the case, so that in this limited aspect the despised pidgin languages are more advanced than such cherished forms of speech as classical Sanskrit. Certainly, then, the evolution of language as such has never been demonstrated, and the inherent equality of all languages must be maintained on present evidence.[7] Yet in the broader sense some correlation between communication and the evolution of culture can be discerned, and language evolves by begetting that which is not language but transcends it, even while it is dependent upon it.

7. Languages are equal in the sense that they are all "created equal," that is, have equal potentialities. In fact, some which have undergone cultivation probably have greater resources of expression, but this is not owing to any inherent superiority. Any language placed in the same position through non-linguistic factors will be capable of similar development.

CHAPTER VI

LANGUAGE, DIFFUSION, AND MIGRATION

LASSIFICATION based on common origin is, as has been seen, fundamental for historical and comparative linguistics. Its importance is so obvious that when language classification is referred to without further qualification, it is genetic comparison that is normally meant. Yet there are other equally legitimate methods of language classification useful for other purposes. Confusion results only when a classification reached by one method is erroneously treated as an exemplification of one of the other methods, thus leading to invalid inferences.

There are three methods of language classification which are of major significance: the genetic, the typological, and the areal. Of these, the genetic is the only one which is at once non-arbitrary, exhaustive, and unique. By "non-arbitrary" is here meant that there is no choice of criteria leading to different and equally legitimate results. This is because genetic classification reflects historical events which must have occurred or not occurred. If the classification is correct, it implies events which did occur. By "exhaustiveness" of a classification is meant that all languages are put into some class, and by "uniqueness" that no language is put into more than one class. Genetic classification, as has been seen, is based on criteria of sound-meaning resemblances of linguistic forms. Related languages are likely to be in the same geographical region but usually are not in continuous distribution. In principle, geography is irrelevant, although it is a normal result that related languages are in the same general area. This is a reflection of the types of populational movements which have in fact occurred in the past. The present distribution of English with substantial communities on four continents is, in turn, a reflection of new conditions of communication of relatively recent date. Were people to be discovered on the moon speaking a language with the vocabulary and grammar of English, a conclusion of genetic relationship would perforce be drawn, regardless of geographical circumstances.

Typological classifications are based on criteria of sound without meaning, meaning without sound, or both. For example, using a phonetic criterion only, we might divide the languages of the world into two typological classes, those with tonal systems and those lacking tonal systems. Both classes would be extensive, but the latter would be larger. Using a semantic feature only, one might divide the languages of the world into those which have morphemes indicating sex gender and those which do not. We could combine the two criteria mentioned to produce four classes of languages: tonal–gender, tonal–non-gender, non-tonal–gender, and non-tonal–non-gender. Typological classifications are arbitrary because any criterion or combination of criteria may be used with consistent results, provided only that they have clear meaning when applied to diverse languages. Some classes may be empty. This would be so if, for example, there were no tonal languages with sex gender in this classification. As we increase the number of criteria, we increase the number of possible classes and decrease the membership of each until each language becomes a separate type. On the other hand, if we divide languages into those with vowels and those without vowels, all the languages of the world will be in the first class, while the second will be empty. The methodological likeness of typological to racial classification based on phenotypic characteristics is obvious. Many trivial and pointless classifications into language types are possible. We attempt to set up significant classifications by choosing criteria which tend to cluster together and involve linguistic traits judged to have fundamental significance. For all its other vital weaknesses, the nineteenth-century classification of languages into isolating, agglutinative, and inflective fulfilled this requirement.

Typological classifications are arbitrary, as has just been indicated, exhaustive, and unique. They have no necessary historical implications. There is in most cases a tendency for genetically related languages to belong to the same type, but there will generally be exceptions. Moreover, many genetically unrelated languages will belong to the same type. A typological and genetic classification will probably never agree even for a restricted area. The use of criteria relevant only for typologic classifications to establish supposed genetic families is widespread. Since typologies are arbitrary, the result will be apparent discrepancies when two or more writers employ distinct typological criteria. Virtually all discrepant classifications result from the conflict between a number of purely typological classifications or between a true genetic classification and several typological ones. In the interests of scientific clarity, such terms as "family" and "relationship" should be confined entirely to their traditional reference to genetic classifications. Typological classes of languages are geographically discontinuous, and the same class is likely to have representatives in many different parts of the world.

Areal classifications are based on effects of languages upon one another, whether they are related or unrelated. Among the relevant data are borrowings, involving both sound and meaning, and influences in sound only or meaning only which are the result of historical contact. A number of languages which share many such features with one another may be called an "areal group." To avoid confusion, it seems advisable, as mentioned previously, to confine the use of the terms "family" and "relationship" to genetically connected languages. We may then talk of genetic families, typological classes, and areal groups.

Areal classifications depend on judgments that certain languages have affected one another more than each has influenced, or been influenced by, languages outside the group. Since languages in contact practically always affect one another in some way, this requires, in general, a decision as to whether a particular language has influenced some one language more than another. This, in turn, requires a weighting of judgments, some of them uncertain, about essentially separate and disparate traits. Areal classifications are therefore arbitrary within limits. They are neither exhaustive nor unique. If a language has neither received nor exerted significant influence, a situation quite conceivable through geographical isolation or recency of arrival in an area, it cannot be assigned to any group. It might, however, as a limiting case, be considered a group by itself. It also happens that a language shows mutual influences with two groups of languages which have not affected each other. Such a language is likely to be geographically intermediate. It might then be assigned to both groups or be considered marginal. Areal groups are, almost necessarily, geographically continuous.

The resemblance of areal groups of languages to culture areas has perhaps already occurred to the reader. Both cover geographically continuous areas and are typically considered the result of diffusional influences within a restricted region. There is the same quasi-arbitrariness of classification and even the close parallel of marginal languages to marginal cultures. Since the same contacts which lead to cultural diffusion in general must lead to linguistic diffusion, it may be expected that classifications into linguistic areal groups will closely parallel culture-area classifications. Therefore, linguistic criteria relevant to language-area grouping can well be employed alongside the usual non-linguistic criteria in determining culture areas.

In the past this has not been done. In discussions by anthropologists of culture areas, the comparison with linguistic data, if made at all, is with genetic classifications. Agreements and disagreements between culture areas and genetic language areas as found on the usual language maps are then noted. The degree of congruence is often not high or is even non-existent. In a sense a genetic distribution can be considered to consist of the scattered members of portions of former culture areas. Related languages are the historical continuations of a single ancestral language which once, usually some thousands of years ago, was spoken by a culturally unified community in a continuous area. Even at that time, to judge by present situations, it is unlikely that such a language community constituted a cultural area by itself. It doubtless shared features based on linguistic contacts with a number of neighboring linguistic communities. It is evident, then, that it is the language area, not the genetic family, which corresponds to the culture area both in the historic processes of its formation and in most formal characteristics.

It has sometimes been suggested that linguistic features be mapped distributionally, as is done with other cultural traits. This is in itself a useful step, but the comparison of such distributions will not immediately result in language areas as defined here. The similarities must first be evaluated as the result of common origin, interlanguage influence, or convergence. Unless such an analysis, which assumes a correct genetic classification and a certain amount of comparative reconstruction as a basis, has been carried out, we shall be lumping together resemblances of diverse origin, and a coherent, meaningful result is not likely to emerge. There is thus no opposition between genetic and areal classification. The former is, instead, a prerequisite for the successful attainment of the latter.

Although it is clear what kinds of data are to be utilized as the basis of linguistic-area classifications, the methodological problem of determining their existence still remains. There are four classes of linguistic contact phenomena to be considered: borrowing, order, semantic influence, and phonologic influence. "Borrowing," in accordance with normal usage, is defined here as the acceptance in one language of a form, in both its sound and its meaning aspects, from another language, though usually with both phonetic and semantic modifications. There are a number of criteria which are usually sufficient to determine the existence of borrowing. The question is, in general, easier of determination if the languages concerned are unrelated, since in this case, of the two common alternative explanations—genetic relationship and chance—the first is eliminated by definition.

With unrelated languages in the absence of written records, the most powerful method is the distribution of forms. That is, we do not take into account merely the two languages concerned but all related and neighboring languages of the original pair. A form with widespread cognates in the languages related to one of the two, but restricted to the language itself or to a few neighboring languages in the language family to which the first language belongs, is surely a borrowing from the first language to the second. Accident is never totally eliminated as a possibility, but the existence of other borrowings between the same languages, particularly in the same semantic sphere, geographical proximity, and the existence of other nonlinguistic evidences of cultural contact all add to the probability that the resemblance is not accidental. More purely linguistic factors are the length of the form and the presence of sound correspondences recurrent in other presumed borrowings. Another criterion is based on the sounds contained in the form. For example, words in Berber which contain ḥ are borrowed from Arabic. Even without the other considerations which point in this direction, the fact that there are no words in Berber containing ḥ without similar words in Arabic but that there are many Arabic words containing ḥ for which nothing corresponding exists in Berber is sufficient.

Between related languages all the foregoing considerations hold, but the addition of genetic relationship as a possible explanation complicates the picture. It also brings with it, however, the possibility of applying reconstructive techniques. If correspondences are of the type found in cognates, then common origin rather than borrowing is the explanation. This is not always sufficient in itself. For example, Hausa, which is ultimately related to Arabic in the Afroasiatic family, has also been under strong direct influence from the latter. The form *mútù*, "to die," shows correspondences characteristic both of inherited cognates and of borrowed forms to Arabic *(ya)mu·tu*, "(he) dies." Distribution is useful here also. The occurrence of similar forms in literally scores of languages of the Chad group of Afroasiatic, to which Hausa belongs, in the language of many groups not subject to Arab influence makes the case for borrowing far less compelling. Its appearance in fundamental vocabulary also points to common origin as the more probable explanation. The negative argument is much stronger. The absence of forms corresponding to Hausa *yâmmà*, "west" [Arabic *yaman(a)*], from a single language in the Chad group other than

Hausa is a powerful argument against common origin in this case and in favor of borrowing from Arabic.

In principle, resemblances in meaningful order among neighboring languages belong with sound-meaning resemblances. In both instances, there is the combination of a formal aspect with a semantic aspect. Since order allows of far fewer formal possibilities than sound combinations and since meaningful order has typically relational significances linking word classes which are necessarily few in number (possession, goal of action, etc.), the probabilities of chance convergence are considerable.

An inherited construction can be most convincingly established where a particular meaningful order is found in different and geographically disconnected subgroups and where, in each instance, surrounding unrelated languages do not share in the construction. Once the inherited construction can be established, then any divergent construction can be attributed to some change. If the divergent construction coincides with that of neighboring unrelated languages, the possibility of influence as an explanation can be entertained. In view of the limited alternatives, however, even in these cases convergence through internal development cannot be excluded as a possible explanation.

Resemblances in meaning only, as the result of semantic borrowing, are common among both related and unrelated languages. For example, throughout most of Negro Africa there is a single term meaning both "meat" and "animal"; "fruit" is expressed by a phrase meaning "child of the tree"; and "door" is "mouth of the house." Such meaning resemblances are practically always the result either of influence or of convergence.[1] The argument for historical influence is here identical with that for continuously distributed cultural traits. It is improbable, though not impossible, that such a distribution would result from more than a single origin. On the other hand, any such purely semantic trait has always the potentiality of independent origin. For example, the African idiom "mouth of the house" for "door" mentioned here has a fairly continuous distribution in Africa but reappears in Siberia. In dealing with an instance of this kind concerning linguistic data, our probable conclusion is that there were two, but no more than two, separate inventions. Separate inventions (convergence) always seem possible in the realm of meanings. A particular combination of meaning aspects in a single term or a particular phrase with specialized meaning (idiomatic meaning), unless it is an accidental homonym, in which case it has no historic significance, involves an observation of some similarity in phenomena, an implied metaphor, which, if it can be noted by one people, can presumably be noted by another. In this respect it can in nowise be compared to, say, the plot of an entire story involving a complex of accidents, but it is rather like some single folklore motif which may be easily duplicated.

1. Strictly speaking, one might say that meanings could be genetically related without any connection in sound. If, for example, two languages retained a complete set of kin terms, with the same meanings as a continuation of the same kinship system in the ancestral language community, but if in every case there had been replacement by new sequences of phonemes, one could say that the meanings were historically connected but not the sounds.

Influence of sound systems on one another remains to be considered. There are two chief mechanisms involved here: the presence of the foreign sound in borrowed words and sound changes by which an earlier sound is replaced by one which is part of the regular system of a neighboring language. This latter phenomenon presumably happens most easily through the influence of bilingual speakers, who in their "accent" replace the traditional sound by that of the neighboring tongue which they speak as their first language. The presence of sounds originating in another language through borrowings is easily ascertainable as an incidental result of the study of borrowings, as noted previously. The relative rarity of the phoneme in the borrowing language, combined with its occurrence exclusively, or almost exclusively, in words which occur in the donor language also, constitutes decisive evidence. It is sometimes held that borrowings will incorporate sounds not found previously in the language of the borrowers only if there is already a "gap" in the system ready to be filled; otherwise there will be a substitution of some inherited sound. For example, the ease with which English maintained the French $\check{z}$ sound in borrowed words is explained by the fact that English already had both an unvoiced counterpart $\check{s}$ and the pattern of phonemic contrast of voiced versus unvoiced phonemes, e.g., $s:z$, $t:d$, etc. This is doubtless a factor, but not the only one, since there are well-attested cases of foreign sounds incorporated through borrowings for which no such preparatory situation exists, for example, the click sounds in Zulu and other Bantu languages in words borrowed from Khoisan languages.

Externally induced sound changes resulting in a sound system more like that of the influencing language can be inferred after the event only on a probability basis. There is no general sound change externally caused which could not potentially result from internal development. The rarer the change on a world-wide basis and in other languages of the same family, the more unlikely that it should occur purely through internal causation in just such a fashion that the sound system, after the change has been accomplished, approximates more closely than before that of a neighboring language. The existence of several such changes in the sound system accompanied by other evidences of language contact, e.g., borrowing, greatly increases the probability of such an interpretation.

The total effect of such interinfluencing of sound systems in a given area over a long period can be very striking; even unrelated languages come to have almost identical sound systems, as, for example, among the aboriginal languages of the northwest coast of the United States and the neighboring areas of Canada. Much of the confusion which has enveloped the discussion of the origin of this situation in the area arises from the assumption, rejected earlier in the discussion of genetic relationship, that resemblances in the sound system as such are evidence for genetic relationship. Once attention is concentrated on sound-meaning resemblances, then certain genetic relationships in the area, e.g., Athabascan-Tlingit-Haida, become clear, and others can be rejected. The resemblance or lack of resemblance of the sound systems can then be investigated within the normal frame of established genetic relationships, using the established methods of reconstructing earlier sound systems. The indications are that both genetic inheritance among those languages which are related and influences of the kind discussed here have been instrumental in producing the existing situation.

To sum up, among contact phenomena, borrowing provides the most assured basis, because convergence is excluded for all practical purposes. Borrowings among unrelated languages are the easiest of all to detect. Semantic influence comes next in degree of certainty. Here convergence is a definite, though usually minor, possibility, while the genetic explanation is virtually excluded. Order constructions and sound influences are the most difficult to establish. The presence of many such indications combined with the more certain evidence from borrowing and calques strengthens the case for all, while not lending a very high degree of certainty to any particular instance. Since in outlining areal classifications it is the general fact of language contact which is of interest, not the specific validity of each inference, this will not greatly hamper the actual work of areal classification.

The culture area is primarily a diffusionist concept. Diffusionist approaches have sometimes been treated as virtual equivalents of migrational theories. Historically they are connected, in that both types assumed prominence at the same time as a methodological weapon against nineteenth-century evolutionism through the explanation of cultural resemblances by the mechanism of historical connections originating in the movements of cultural features. Methodologically, however, the resemblances are superficial. This becomes particularly clear when the linguistic counterparts of each type of theory are considered.

The most consistent and fully elaborated migrational theory is that of the *Kulturkreislehre* of Central Europe.[2] Prominent members of this school are Graebner, considered the founder, Ankermann, Foy, Schmidt, and Koppers. The fundamental methodological concept of this school is the *Kulturkreis*, literally translated "culture circle." *Kulturkreise* are established through certain kinds of cultural similarities, summed up in the two criteria of quality and quantity, which may be briefly described as follows.

Quality refers to the comparison of individual traits from the two or more cultures which are to be demonstrated as representatives of the same *Kreise*. For each such individual trait, e.g., house type, a qualitative comparison will distinguish features which are largely independent of one another and not determined by the function of the material trait or institution. For example, house types can be compared for ground plan, material used, form of the roof, decorations, number and kinds of entrances, etc. If a number of such qualitative resemblances are found, the application of the qualitative criterion has led to a conclusion of historical connection. The quantitative criterion refers to the presence of convincing qualitative resemblances in a number of different traits of culture. The applicability of the quantitative criterion strengthens the case for each of the qualitative resemblances, for, it is argued,

2. Basic expositions of the *Kulturkreis* point of view are F. Graebner, *Methode der Ethnologie* (Heidelberg, 1911), and W. Schmidt, *The Cultural Historical Method of Ethnology*, trans. S. A. Sieber (New York, 1939).

two peoples might conceivably, however unlikely the case, arrive independently at two house types which shared a large number of qualitative similarities; what practically excludes chance is the same phenomenon in a series of different traits: house types, weapons, musical instruments, social organization, religion, etc. It is claimed by proponents of the school that the same *Kreise* can be discovered in various parts of the world—Asia, Oceania, Africa, and South America. The explanation is a series of migrations from Asiatic centers.

The parallelism of this method to that of the establishing of genetic relationship among languages as described in a previous chapter is obvious. Comparing single forms in two languages to reveal specific points of comparison in sound corresponds to the criterion of quality—for example, the comparison of English "hound" and German *Hund*. The existence of a large number of such qualitative resemblances between two languages is the application of the criterion of quantity. The *Kulturkreis* procedure is therefore the methodological parallel of the genetic method in linguistics, and *Kulturkreise* are essentially genetically related cultures. Thus, on the one hand, culture area, diffusion, and linguistic areal classification correspond and, on the other, *Kulturkreis*, migration, and linguistic genetic classification.

Just as in the course of linguistic genetic procedure, resemblances between contiguous non-related languages are to be explained by the disturbing factor of contact or borrowing, so, where traits supposedly diagnostic of one *Kulturkreis* are found in a culture assigned to another *Kreis*, the explanation must be diffusion, the cultural analogue of borrowing. Thus the *Kulturkreislehre*, far from being a diffusionist theory, finds in diffusion its chief methodological source of disturbance. The irrelevance of geographical separation to hypotheses of genetic relationship has been noted. It is this realization which underlies the insistence of exponents of the *Kulturkreislehre* that distance is irrelevant; that, if certain cultural resemblances obtain, common cultural origin through affiliation with the same *Kreis* is the only possible explanation.

It is of some interest to note that Graebner, the founder of the school, is aware in his classical *Methode* of some resemblance between his method and that of comparative linguistics. However, he equates the criterion of quantity with vocabulary resemblance and that of form or quality with similarity in grammar. Schmidt, for whom linguistics is a major field of interest, likewise misses the essential parallel. Indeed, in his own linguistic work he frequently abandons normal genetic methods in favor of arbitrarily applied typological criteria, in order to demonstrate a literal agreement between his *Sprachenkreise* and *Kulturkreise*, e.g., in his classification of Australian languages.

Language provides a far more favorable ground for the application of genetic procedures than does a non-linguistic culture. A language consists of a large number of fundamentally independent features, the individual forms. Since, in principle, the relation between sound and meaning, corresponding to form and function, respectively, is arbitrary, the number of different ways in which the same function can be carried out is very large, contrasted with the limitations set by function in most aspects of non-linguistic culture. Furthermore, there is a central core of basic vocabulary and grammatical elements in language which is strongly resistant to outside influence. No comparable barrier against diffusion appears to exist in culture. Likewise, language is, by general consent, impervious to the natural environmental influences which help to produce convergence in non-linguistic culture. Since with all these factors favorable to the application of the genetic method in languages we still arrive at many distinct families and none of the wholesale connections between distant regions, such as South America and Africa, there is the a fortiori probability that the extensive cultural relationships asserted by the adherents of the *Kulturkreislehre* are false.

In this, as in certain other instances discussed in this book, the application of cultural theories to language assists in their clarification. The peculiarities of language, as contrasted with other aspects of culture or with culture as a whole, which often prevent the same degree of success, must be kept in mind. Of these, the most important are the systematic nature of language, the arbitrariness of the relation between form and function, and the lack of relation between language and external environment.

CHAPTER VII

STRUCTURE AND FUNCTION IN LANGUAGE

LIKE evolution, function is a complex idea with varied applications, chiefly in mathematics, biology, and the social sciences. In mathematics a function is a relation between two sets of elements—usually, but not necessarily, numbers—connected by a functional rule which assigns to each member of the first set, called the "argument" or "independent variable," a single member of the second set, called the "value" or the "dependent variable." The second set is said to be the "function" of the first. For example, in the function expressed by $y = x^2$, the sets of values of x are the arguments and those of y the values, so that y is the function of x. This function assigns, for example, to the argument $x = 2$ the value $y = 4$. The same value may be assigned to different arguments, as in the foregoing example, where the value $y = 4$ is assigned to the two different arguments $x = 2$ and $x = -2$.[1] Another way of stating this is to say that a function is a many-one relation. One feature occurring in other subject matter that appears to derive from mathematical usage is the asymmetry of the relation, the values and arguments belonging, in general, to different sets. Important likewise are the notions of predictability—given the functional rule and an argument, the value can be found—and that of the functional dependence of the dependent upon the independent variable. For the special case of one-to-one relations, either x can be stated as a function of y or y as a function of x. For example, in $y = 2x$, which is one-to-one, since every value of y has only one value of x as an argument, we obtain an inverse function $x = y/2$, in which, formally, y is now the function of x. Such one-to-one functions are common in the physical sciences as an expression of a relation between variables. This corresponds to such notions in the social sciences as functional interdependence or concomitant variation, even where, as is often the case, no quantitative values can be assigned to the variables.

Another trait probably derived from mathematical usage is the employment of the phrase "the function." Just as in mathematics a function assigns a single unambiguous value to each argument, so there is a tendency, in spite of the admission of multiple functions by functional theorists, to seek for a single functional answer. What may be considered the functional question par excellence is often put this way: "What is the function of x?" where x stands for some social institution, custom, or item of material culture.

Although functional theory in the social sciences is in the first instance an appli-

1. However, some would include under the term "function" many-valued functions in which the same argument may have more than one value.

cation of the biological, rather than the mathematical, concept of function, it is worth noting that the mathematical usage occurs quite often, even with functionalist writers. Thus when Durkheim states that suicide is a function of lack of organic solidarity, what is meant is that suicide and organic solidarity vary inversely and that suicide is the dependent variable. The assignment of the dependent variable in such cases seems to depend on the diachronic hypothesis that changes in the independent variables precede in time changes in the dependent variable, whether in the same direction as direct variation or in the opposite direction as inverse variation.

Writers who stress a functional approach in the social sciences generally have an analogy from organic life in mind, often explicitly, as in the instances of Durkheim and Radcliffe-Brown, who talk of social morphology and social physiology. We may take the latter's formulation of the biological concept of function stated in a form intended for applicability to the social sciences as a convenient point of departure: "The concept of function as here defined thus involves the notion of a structure consisting of a set of relations amongst unit entities, the continuity of the structure being maintained by a life process made up of the activities of the constituent units."[2] The function of any activity, then, becomes the contribution to the maintenance of the functioning of the structure as a whole, that is, to its necessary conditions of existence. Stated in biological units, an organism has a structure which consists of relations among its constituent parts, the organs. The function of the activity of any organ—for example, seeing—is stated in terms of such contributions to the continued life-process of the total organism as detection of enemies and the noting of sources of nourishment.

A different, but at least equally common, biological use of "function" would identify it with the term "activity" of the foregoing statement. An example of this usage in biology is the statement that the function of the eye is seeing. Radcliffe-Brown specifically disclaims this meaning of "function" in the social sciences and in a recent publication proposes to call it "process."[3] In practice, however, this usage is fairly frequent among anthropological writers, even functionalists, who in such instances are lapsing into the everyday use of the term. An example would be the statement that among certain people clans have the function of distributing lands. In terms of the foregoing paradigm, land distribution is rather an activity whose function we then investigate.

Where it is necessary to distinguish, the term "organic function" will be applied to this latter usage, since it corresponds to the attribution of function to an organ, while "activity function" will designate those instances in which the function of the activity is being considered. Thus seeing is an organic function of the eye; protection from enemies is an activity function of seeing. Note that even if we accept activity functioning as the standard interpretation for the social sciences, the existence of

2. A. R. Radcliffe-Brown, "On the Concept of Function in Social Science," originally published in 1935, reprinted in his *Structure and Function in Primitive Society* (London, 1952), p. 180.

3. *Structure and Function in Primitive Society*, p. 12.

something which has the activity, corresponding to the organ in biology, is implied, and its identification is germane to the analysis as a whole.

A third type of functioning is that in which the functional effects of the unit's activities are not considered in their bearing on the functioning of the total structure but rather on that of some other part which participates in the same structure. This may be called "internal function." In biology the circulatory system, which, among other activities, brings the material from which muscle fibers are maintained, is internal in its function.

From the fact that an arrangement is not considered functional except in relation to a structure of some duration, it is useful to abstract from time as long as analysis is centered on the functions of a specific structure. The study of language here furnishes an example; the major subdiscipline of descriptive linguistics receives its very possibility of existence from the assumption that language is a structure and that changes which occur over a short period are so negligible that they can be disregarded. The indifference to historical considerations that is typical of more extreme functionalist positions arises out of the view that function is a complete explanation;[4] for in this event we may consider a functional arrangement as self-contained and need not inquire into the causes which produced it as a whole in the first instance. Everything is "explained" by its position in the structure and its functioning—what more sophisticated functionalist writers maintain is rather the separateness of these two types of inquiry.[5] The knowledge of functional arrangements produces a kind of precarious predictability which is much employed in the affairs of everyday life—in fact, without which the rational ordering of existence would be impossible.

Thus a continuing functional nexus exists involving an individual, his bank, and the withdrawal of deposited funds, which allows of prediction. It will break down, however, if the bank has failed the previous day, thus dissolving the functional arrangement.

In organic functioning the repeated occurrence of similar effects through the activity of the same unit implies a causal mechanism. In traditional Aristotelian terminology, the organ is the efficient cause of the activity, while in activity functioning the traditional causal explanation would be in terms of final causes. Functionalist writers have generally warned that purpose and function need not coincide; only if the effects are those intended, are purpose and function the same. Merton has conceptualized this distinction in the terms "manifest function" where this agreement exists and "latent function" when it is absent.[6]

4. "The explanation of the South Sea outrigger may be found in the fact that this arrangement gives the greatest stability, seaworthiness and manageability, considering the limitations in material and in technical handicraft of the Oceanic cultures" (B. Malinowski, "Culture" in *Encyclopaedia of the Social Sciences*, IV [1935], 627). Even here history enters the back door in the final qualifying clause.

5. Cf. Durkheim: "When the explanation of a social phenomenon is undertaken, we must separately seek the efficient cause which produces it and the function which it fulfills" (*The Rules of Sociological Method*, trans. S. A. Solovay and J. H. Mueller [8th ed.; Chicago, 1938], p. 95).

6. R. Merton, *Social Theory and Social Structure* (Glencoe, Ill., 1949).

Distinct from the afore-mentioned causal factors inherent in the functional arrangement are the causes of the functional arrangement as a whole. For the latter there are obviously historical factors which figure in a complete explanation. The same function can always be performed by alternate structures, though only a limited variety of such structures is possible. Hence the mere fact that a particular function is performed is not sufficient to account for the specific structural arrangement. We therefore consider it in relation to its historical antecedents. We also investigate functional alternatives on a comparative basis, in order to discover the range of possible structures capable of fulfilling a given function.

The consideration of functional alternatives brings with it, inevitably, the related concept of functional efficiency. We can compare diverse structures with the same or similar functions with regard to the effectiveness with which the function is performed. The close connection of functional and evolutionary theory at this point was noted in a previous chapter. While not logically necessitated by a study of relative functional efficiency, the evolutionary theory that, of alternative structures, those tend to become dominant in the long run which are most efficient is likely to be suggested by the comparative study of similarly functioning structures and can be stated only in terms of such comparison.

There is a strong tendency in functional studies to assume that all activities make positive contributions to the continuance of the total structure. From this point of view an activity can be positively functional, negatively functional (dysfunctional), or functionally indifferent. There is a reasonable basis, however, if not for the assumption of the universally positive effect of all activities, then of a total balance in favor of positive function within any given structure, inasmuch as the very survival of the structure up to the moment of investigation suggests such a preponderance of positive factors.

The application of the biologic concept of function, which has just been discussed, to sociocultural phenomena raises some specific problems. The most obvious choice of a whole corresponding to the organism in biology is, no doubt, the society, in terms of whose necessary conditions of existence the functions of activities are to be discovered. But, in order to apply the functional paradigm, the whole must be endowed with a structure consisting of parts in stable relations to one another and characterized by activities relevant to the whole. In biology the part, an organ, is given in a clear-cut manner as a quasi-permanent arrangement of matter, while its activity is some repeated change or movement. In biological study we usually first note the organ as given and then investigate its activities and the relevance of these activities to the life-process of the organism. There are even easily identifiable organs, such as the appendix, with no discoverable activity and others with activities as yet partly undiscovered—for example, the ductless glands.

In human society a social group smaller than the society as a whole has some of the properties of quasi-permanence and definiteness of outline which mark the organ in biology. However, in contrast to the biological analogy, we usually discover and define the unit through the distinctiveness of its activity. In a few instances, such as the nuclear family, a group can be defined in terms other than its cultural activities; in such cases we may first specify the unit and then explore its possible activities and their functions.

The key part played by the concept of social structure in contemporary British social anthropology and stemming from Radcliffe-Brown seems to arise from the consideration that if there is function, there must be a functioning structure, the two concepts being correlative, and that only social groups are capable of satisfying this requirement. At this point there is an interesting and instructive divergence from Malinowski, in whose thinking it is rather the institution, defined as an organized set of cultural activities, which becomes the basic structural unit. Malinowski's penchant for stressing individual rather than social needs, though not to the exclusion of the latter, points to still further possible sources of ambiguity in functionalist studies. The structural whole may conceivably be different from what may be called the "whole of reference," that is, the whole in terms of whose needs functions are to be investigated. Thus the relevance of the activities of social units, considered as a part of society structurally, may be considered in reference to the necessary conditions of existence of the individual, of some social unit smaller than the society or even some body of organized cultural behavior, e.g., religion. The failure to specify the whole of reference is an occasional source of obscurity in functional studies. Even in biology, it may be noted, activities can be considered according to their functional relevance to the survival of the species as well as to that of the individual, often with very different conclusions as to their positive or negative functional value.

It has been seen that the functional question, to be meaningful, requires the specification of a whole of reference. This whole may in turn be viewed as part of a larger structure and the functions of its activities in this wider context investigated, thus producing a functional chain. For example, in biology we do not normally inquire into the functions of a beaver's activities, but if some larger whole is specified, this becomes a meaningful question. We may, for example, consider the beaver in relation to the ecology of a particular region. The higher the unit in a functional chain, the more extensive and diffuse are its effects and the more difficult it becomes to discover the necessary conditions of existence to which its activities are to be related. One methodological approach that suggests itself is the comparative. A comparison of religious behavior among various cultural groups suggests that the functions of religion as a whole, which are so difficult to isolate in a single society, may be clarified through cross-cultural investigations. The reasoning is tacitly negative. If something is not found everywhere in connection with religion, it is evidently not essential and therefore probably not a part which contributes to the functional effect of religion as a whole. What is not eliminated by this procedure is a religious universal; and the converse conclusion is drawn, whether correctly or not, that whatever is effected by such activity is a function of religion everywhere. So, if we did not know the organic function of an automobile as motion and noted that, whereas some had radios and some had not, all had engines, a study of the activity of the engine would shed light on the over-all function of the automobile.

Keeping in mind the multiplicity of functional paradigms—organic, activity, and internal—and the variety of possible identifications of structural wholes and wholes of reference, it is not surprising that quite disparate statements regarding the function of language or of aspects of language should exist. Such approaches are not necessarily incompatible when it is realized that "function" is a term which, as has been seen, covers a great range of possible researches in regard to the same general subject matter.

Thus Malinowski elaborates a functional approach to language which seems concerned with its semantic aspects alone and which may be summed up in the assertion that the meaning of words is what they effect in a cultural context: "The meaning of words consists in what they achieve by concerted action, the indirect handling of the environment through direct action upon the organism."[7] A more complex analysis, which also takes the speech utterance as its unit, is that of Bühler, who proposes a threefold division of linguistic science founded on three functions inherent in the speech situation.[8] An utterance has, with reference to the speaker, the contents, and the hearer, respectively, an expressive, a representational, and a pragmatic function. This latter refers to the modification of the behavior of the listener by the utterance. Of the same general type is the current distinction between emotional and referential functions of words, first introduced by Ogden and Richards.[9]

Another class of statement is that of sociologists and anthropologists regarding the function of language in providing a system of communication as a precondition for widespread social co-operation and in making possible cultural accumulation. Here belong Herskovits' characterization of language as the vehicle of culture and Levy's requirement of a communication system as a functional prerequisite for a society.[10]

The statements thus far considered, all of them by non-linguists, concern the functional role of language as a part within a larger totality of society or cultural behavior. It is natural that the total structure with which linguists tend to work should be language itself, and the type of functioning considered will be that of units of linguistic structure in reference to the total structure of the language. In the present terminology it can be stated as roughly true that non-linguists have been concerned with the external functioning of language, linguists with its internal functioning.

The various contemporary approaches to linguistics seem to have as their com-

7. Malinowski, *op. cit.*, p. 622.

8. K. Bühler, *Sprachtheorie* (Jena, 1934), p. 28.

9. C. K. Ogden and I. A. Richards, *The Meaning of Meaning* (New York, 1923).

10. M. J. Herskovits, *Cultural Anthropology* (New York, 1955), pp. 287 ff.; and M. J. Levy, *The Structure of Society* (Princeton, 1952).

mon denominator an emphasis on structure as the master concept, and structure, as we have seen, is correlative with function. Probably the most common version of the phoneme concept has been that in which the phoneme is defined with reference to its functional potentiality for distinguishing meanings. For example, in the programmatic statements of the Prague School, the very existence of units is held to consist in their functioning within a system for differentiating meaning. The extent to which contrasts between any two particular phonemes actually realize this potentiality, its *rendement fonctionelle*, is declared to be a subject for quantitative investigation and is also considered relevant to an understanding of the dynamics of changes in phonologic systems.[11]

The hierarchical organization of language carries with it the possibility of posing functional problems by treating each level as a substructure in its own right. The existence of discrete countable units in grammar and phonology allows the investigation of the functioning efficiency of such substructures in terms of their relevance to the over-all function of language in communication by appropriate mathematical

TABLE 4

	Bilabial	Alveolar
Voiced non-nasal...........	b	d
Voiced nasal...............	m	n
Unvoiced non-nasal........	p	t
Unvoiced nasal............	M	N

techniques. Some of these possibilities have, of course, been explored without explicit recognition of their functional character. The value of a functional approach to language would seem to lie not in any attempt to explain phenomena by the functions they perform but in the heuristic service it may perform in systematically specifying areas of research by raising problems of function and functional efficiency. In what follows, a few of these possibilities are outlined, in order to give some indication of their nature and scope.

Thus, at the lowest level of phonology, the phonemes may be considered substructures, of which the parts are the so-called features, such as bilabial articulation, voicing, etc. One type of investigation is the measurement of the functional efficiency of a phonemic system by employing the mathematical techniques of information theory. That system is most efficient in which all the combinations of features are utilized. If, for example, a language employs a distinctive contrast of nasal articulation and non-nasal articulation, of bilabial and alveolar stops, and of voicing and unvoicing, the most efficient use of these resources will allow of eight phonemes (see Table 4).

11. An early statement may be found in the "Projet de terminologie standardisée," *Travaux du Cercle linguistique de Prague*, Vol. IV (1931). Phonology is defined here as the "part of linguistics treating of phonetic phenomena from the point of view of their functions in language." The sixth of eight basic questions laid down is: "What is the functional load of the various phonologic oppositions?"

A language which, like English, does not have unvoiced nasals, although the contrast of voiced and unvoiced sounds is used otherwise, is inefficient in this respect. What, however, is efficient in this respect may be dysfunctional when considered on the higher structural level of complete utterances, where utilization of every resource of features would lead to insufficient redundancy. The full use of every possibility of contrast would bring it about that lapses would far more frequently produce other meaningful combinations than utterances outside the system, thus increasing the possibilities of failure in communication. We might hypothesize, therefore, that some middle value would appear in languages as a compromise between the two functional requirements.

A recent study by Soporta treats sequences of phonemes, in this instance consonants, from a similar point of view.[12] The number of features by which adjacent consonants differ is treated as a probable compromise between the demands of the speaker for ease of articulation, which reduces this distance, and that of the hearer for distinctness of articulation, which increases it.

Studies of the degree of actual utilization of potential sources of contrast for each pair of phonemes have been mentioned. Again, from the relative frequency of individual phonemes and phoneme sequences, measures of entropy for the phoneme systems as a whole can be derived through information-theory techniques. The degree of allophonic variation existing in language is still another problem of functional phonemics.

Questions of morphological functioning have as yet been little studied. One problem concerns the degree of tolerance of morphological irregularities. An irregular alternation bears no semantic function in so far as it involves a variation in form which does not distinguish meaning, although a function in increasing redundancy might be admitted. Thus the alternation *keep* or *kep-* in English does not distinguish meaning, since the past is already expressed by *-t*. The degree of morphologic irregularity can be measured by the ratio of irregular to regular constructions in samples of text.[13] Another field of investigation is in regard to the phonemic composition of morphemes. The extent of what Hockett has called "canonic form," that is, the presence of standard types of phoneme and the sequence for each class of morphemes, can be studied. A well-known example is the general Semitic rule that verb-root morphemes shall consist of a sequence of three consonants. Investigation of patterns of allowed or forbidden similarities belongs here. To cite once more the example of Semitic, consonants with the same point of articulation occur with far less than chance frequency in the same verbal root, and many possibilities do not occur at all.[14]

Likewise, morpheme length can be subject to study. Excess of either shortness or

12. S. Soporta, "Frequency of Consonant Clusters," *Language*, XXXI (1955), 25–30.

13. This method is described under the name "agglutination index" in J. H. Greenberg, "A Quantitative Approach to the Morphological Typology of Language," in R. F. Spencer (ed.), *Methods and Perspectives in Anthropology* (Minneapolis, 1954).

14. J. Cantineau, "Esquisse d'une phonologie de l'Arabe classique," *Bulletin de la Société Linguistique de Paris*, CXXVI (1946), 93–140; and J. H. Greenberg, "The Patterning of Root Morphemes in Semitic," *Word*, VI (1950), 162–81.

length seems to be avoided. Similar considerations apply to word length, which can be analyzed in reference to both the number of constituent phonemes and the constituent morphemes.

Functional syntactic problems have been dealt with widely in quantitative stylistics, discourse analysis, and word-frequency studies such as those initiated by Zipf. The relatively high degree of development of this area as compared with morphology probably rests on the fact that studies of this kind, being marginal to linguistics as usually practiced, have for the most part been undertaken by non-linguists, who have taken the definition and internal structure of the word for granted and utilized it as their basic unit.

The semantic problem of ambiguity, of which homonymity of words is a particular example, may, in a sense, be considered the obverse of morphological irregularity. In irregular alternation in morphology several forms fulfil the same function, while in ambiguity the same form fulfils several functions. The degree to which homonyms may be tolerated without a risk of breakdown in communication is a problem in functional semantics. The extent of patterning in the semantic field is another area of investigation. For example, some degree of organization seems to be required for a numeral system of indefinite extension, if only because the numerals are transfinite in number while a language can have only a finite number of morphemes. Here, as in other aspects of semantic investigation, the absence of a methodology comparable to that of phonology and grammar hinders the precise formulation of problems.

The semantic topics just mentioned pertain to the meaning of linguistic units and constructions smaller than the sentence. Like the phonological and morphological investigations mentioned previously, they belong to the realm of internal linguistic functioning, although their indirect bearing on the actual efficiency of communication is involved in every case. It is only with the level of sentential meaning that we encounter the external functioning of language.

At this point, however, confusion is likely to arise unless two senses of sentential meaning are distinguished.[15] The meanings of units, such as words, and of constructions contained within the sentence are described in ordinary grammatical and lexicographic studies by reference to their function within the sentence. The meaning of a sentence in one sense, here called the "internal meaning," is the resultant of the meanings of all its constituent units and constructions. Hence two occurrences of the "same" sentence, that is, the same in consisting of the same units in the same order, necessarily have the same internal meaning. However, these distinct occurrences may have very different functional effects in different situations. They may therefore be said to have different "external" meanings. The following example may help in clarifying this distinction. The "same" sentence, "The window is open,"

---

15. The distinction between two kinds of sentential meaning made here is also to be found in C. Fries, "Meaning in Linguistic Analysis," *Language*, XXX (1954), 57–68, in which the term "linguistic meaning" corresponds to the "internal meaning" of this work and "social-cultural meaning" to "external meaning."

functions as a very different stimulus to behavior if said by someone in a room on a cold day or if recited as part of the stage directions for a scene by the director of a play. The internal meanings of the two occurrences are here the same, the external meanings different.

Such classifications as those of Bühler into expressive, representational, and pragmatic functions and such categories as the cognitive, emotive, and aesthetic functions of language are general classes of external functions. Numerous classifications are possible here. Without any attempt at exhaustiveness or precision, one may specify the external functions of giving information, affecting the behavior of individuals, setting up social bonds (Malinowski's "phatic communion"), aesthetic expression, humor, and magical activity. The total effect of all external functions is sometimes called "communication" and includes in this aesthetic and emotional expressions as well as the total effect of conveyance of information. The common statement that the function of language is communication is, then, a statement of the function of language at this level.

At the highest level of all, one may inquire into the functional effects of communication in turn on the society as a whole and its correspondence with social needs. Here belong statements concerning the role of language as communication in integrating the society as a whole, in defining political entities, and in producing widespread social co-ordination. Here also belong the functions of communication in the transmission of culture from one generation to another, in the diffusion of cultural traits from society to society, and in making cultural accumulation possible. The indispensability of language or of a system of similar structure for human culture rests, in the final analysis, on its function in maintaining and transmitting new patterns of activity.

At every level in language it is clear that, given the structure, we cannot predict the function. From the features we cannot predict the phonemes. From the phonemes we cannot predict the combinations which will form elementary units. From the phonemes which compose the units we cannot predict their meaning. This is the well-known principle of the arbitrariness of the relation between sound and meaning. In this case we have seen, in the discussion of linguistic relationship, that, although prediction is not possible, we can in certain cases involving sound symbolism arrive at better than chance results. This is the extreme instance of arbitrariness. In other instances, e.g., the construction of phonemes from features, the possible features are limited, and certain combinations are far more frequent than others. We here arrive once again at the relevance of universals to functional considerations. That universals are not always indispensable and do not always make a positive contribution to the fulfilment of needs is shown by the instances of homonyms and morphological irregularities, which, like Durkheim's crime, are normal but not beneficial. They are, however, the by-products of regular sound change, which obviously has a functional aspect. The great majority of sound changes result in abbreviations of articulatory movements. So even here functional considerations play a role.

Throughout change, functional requirements provide bounds, however wide, outside which language risks a breakdown of communication, and everywhere, among possible alternatives, certain ones are far more frequent than others, suggesting that the reason therefor must be in intimate connection with the over-all work performed by language. As different as languages are, the considerations of the first chapter will show that linguistic structure realizes but an infinitesimal portion of the logical possibilities of interpreted sign systems.

This suggests that it is worth our while to determine what universally characterizes languages among all possible sign systems and what functional connection exists between these characteristics and the operation of the human organism in socially organized groups with shared patterns of behavior. It is this problem with which the final chapter will be concerned.

CHAPTER VIII

ORDER OF AFFIXING: A STUDY IN GENERAL LINGUISTICS

ALONGSIDE the traditional branches of descriptive linguistics and historical linguistics, both concerned with the facts of specific languages and specific language families, there is room within linguistic science for a subdiscipline which, under some such name as "general linguistics," will take as its subject matter the systematic study of language universals. Just as historical linguistics cannot proceed without a preliminary fund of descriptive knowledge regarding the languages whose development in time it seeks to fathom, so general linguistics requires a wide basis of accumulated specific knowledge, both descriptive and historical. But in the same way as it has proved practicable to go ahead with the tasks of historical linguistics long before all the languages of the world have been adequately described, so it is entirely feasible to consider problems of general linguistics, even though the specific aims of both descriptive and historical linguistics are far from completion. What is required is merely a sufficient sample of well-studied languages and well-studied historical developments.

Before proceeding to the specific topic of affixing, which will serve to illustrate the methodology of such a general linguistics, it will prove useful to attempt to delimit more exactly its subject matter, the linguistic universal. It is clear, for example, that if our statements are very specific, that is, refer to a relatively restricted class of facts, very few universals can be asserted. If, as an instance, we ask whether the phonemic contrast between voiced and voiceless consonants familiar to us from English is universal, our answer will be in the negative. Similarly, if our inquiry refers to the existence of grammatical categories of singular and plural in the noun or the universality of tense systems in the verb, it will meet with a negative reply. Should we make our classes of fact more general, our chance of discovering universals increases correspondingly. If, instead of asking whether all languages distinguish voiced from unvoiced consonants, we investigate the more general distinction of vowel and consonant, we receive an affirmative answer. As commonplace as such facts frequently are, they are of general linguistic significance and require some explanation, one which inevitably takes into account functional, psychological, and social factors underlying all language behavior.

Such a fact as the universal occurrence of vowels may be termed a "factual universal," since we state some specific fact about language and investigation reveals its universal occurrence. There are, however, many facts of universal significance which we would not wish to exclude from general linguistic consideration, which are not factual universals in the sense described. Thus not only do all languages have phonemes—a typical factual universal—but we find that there are upper and lower limits to the number of elements in a phonemic system (roughly 10–70). The number of phonemes in phoneme systems is not a factual universal because not all languages have the same number of phonemes. Further detailed study would probably show that there is a kind of normal distribution curve involved, with the modal point somewhere between 30 and 40. Such facts may be stated as frequency distributions in the statistical sense. Still another class of facts of interest to a science of general linguistics is based on more than chance occurrence. We are here concerned with such problems as the following: Given a number of functional alternatives, is one significantly more frequent than others? For example, all languages can express the fact that some object has a certain quality to a higher degree than some other object (comparison). Among the methods found are juxtaposition (A is good; B is bad); a special comparative form of the adjective, as in English (A is *better* than B); a verb meaning "to surpass" (A surpasses B in goodness); an adverb of comparative meaning (A is *more* good than B); a preposition (A is good *compared with* B); or a case form of the noun for the object compared (A is good *B-than*). The comparative frequency of these methods is not at all a matter of pure chance. Such facts require explanation.

There are other instances of non-chance distribution where it is not a question of functional alternatives. We may ask whether certain characteristics of languages are correlated with one another in more than chance fashion—whether, for example, Schmidt is correct in saying that certain languages prefer the order determined-determiner and others the opposite in a number of different constructions: noun-dependent genitive, adjective-noun, preposition-noun. This would entail, for example, the thesis that a language in which the preposition preceded the noun would with more than chance frequency have the dependent genitive follow the noun. Such problems, as well as those of functional alternatives previously mentioned, are obviously typological. The discovery of clusters of characteristics with more than chance mutual adherence provides the groundwork for significant typologies.

The question of sound symbolism is likewise one of more than chance correlation. Since no meaning is expressed by the same sound in every language, this is never a case of factual universals; the problem resolves itself into one of frequency. Thus it is clear from even cursory examination of evidence from many parts of the world that words meaning "mother" tend with far more than random frequency to have nasal consonants and to be reduplicative in form.

For purposes of a science of general linguistics, then, we may broaden our notion of universals in language to include (1) factual universals, (2) universal frequency distributions, and (3) the more than chance frequency of distribution of certain characteristics. All such facts may be said to be of universal scope, in that the facts of all languages are taken into consideration in making them. In fact, not every language, only an adequate sample, is all that is necessary. After all, even the totality of contemporary languages constitutes but a sample of all the languages which have ever existed, and we shall never be adequately informed about more than a minute proportion of all languages.

The facts of universal scope listed under 2 and 3 naturally require the counting of cases and the use of statistical procedures. This raises the problem fundamental to all comparative approaches, as to what constitutes a single case. The solution is particularly clear and straightforward in linguistics. A single case is a single historically connected instance. That this is so may be shown by the *reductio ad absurdum* to which we are led by disregarding this principle. Suppose that we are investigating, as a problem in sound symbolism, the connection between vowel sounds and expressions of size. As instances of the association of high front vowels with smallness, we cite: New Yorkese, "litəl"; Philadelphian, "litəl"; Washingtonian, "litəl"; Clevelandic, "litəl"; Chicagoan, "litəl"; Londonian, "litəl." These will count as six instances as against one for a single instance of a low vowel in a word for "little" in an Australian aboriginal language. If we think this is unfair, we can compensate by citing varying local dialect forms from the same Australian language. All of this is obviously arbitrary and will lead to practically any results we wish. The only discernible solution is to consider as one case a single historically connected instance, whether the connection depends on genetic origin or on borrowing and other contact processes. Granted that many individual instances may be regarded as a single historically connected case, the problem will still arise as to what this case is an instance of. In the example cited previously, there will be no hesitation in assigning the various dialect forms of English to a single example of high front unsounded vowel connected with the meaning "small." This is merely because in this case the vowel has been conservative and is retained in phonetically almost identical form by all the dialects. Had there been divergent developments, as is frequently the case, the question could then be asked as to which form should be chosen as representative. The only non-arbitrary answer would seem to be the reconstructed or directly attested ancestral form in cases of genetically related forms. Where the form has been borrowed, our choice will be the reconstructed form in the source language. Thus contemporary English "father" in a study of sound symbolism will be an example of initial *p* rather than *f*, since it derives ultimately from Proto-Indo-European **pətēr* by regular sound changes which affected all words regardless of their meaning. Along with all cognate forms in Indo-European and forms borrowed from these cognates in other Indo-European or non-Indo-European languages, it will count as a single case of initial *p* on a world-wide basis.

These considerations will indicate how artificial is the attempt of such writers as Radcliffe-Brown to separate genetic-historical studies from comparative investigations whose aim is the discovery of general laws. Since, for the purposes of the latter, a single case is a single historically connected instance, progress is dependent on the solution of historic problems whose results thus enter integrally into comparative studies.

A concrete application will perhaps serve to illustrate the methods and conclusions of a general linguistics such as has just been outlined in general terms. As a graduate student, I can remember that I was extremely struck by the statement of Sapir in his book *Language* that prefixing is far less frequent than suffixing in the languages of the world. The reason for my reaction was largely that linguists so rarely, if ever, make general statements of this kind about "all languages." Moreover, such a fact clearly called for a different sort of explanation from the usual specific historical or structural one. My own experience with languages in different parts of the world agrees with Sapir's observation. In all that follows, it will be assumed to be true. The difficulty of answering questions of this kind other than through general impressions underlines the need for some cataloguing of facts regarding all languages that would permit a reliable answer based on systematically assembled data.

In order to account for facts of this kind, one legitimate line of inquiry is directed toward the general facts of human behavior as studied by the science of psychology. As a general working hypothesis we make the following assumption: The relative rarity of one of a number of alternatives on a world-wide basis is the resultant of two factors, one of origin, the other of survival. A rarer alternative will be chosen less often than other alternatives when speakers form a new construction. In the present instance this will mean, say, that if speakers form a new verb tense, they are less likely to prefix than to suffix the tense afformative. Second, the infrequent alternative, even when chosen, will last a shorter period and tend to be replaced by more frequent alternatives. For example, given a language with both prefix and suffix tenses, the prefix formations are more likely to become obsolescent and be replaced or transformed into non-prefix formations over a period of time. As a hypothesis connecting individual and social behavior, we assume that less frequently chosen alternatives under psychological test conditions will be less frequently produced by individuals and, when they occur, are less likely to be imitated by other members of a speech community. As a corresponding diachronic assumption we posit that those reactions involving high frequency of error and slowness of responses on tests are more likely to be replaced by "easier" reactions in the course of language change.

A number of psychological factors will now be adduced which, in general, favor suffixing over prefixing. The first such factor is that which Osgood, summarizing the literature concerning the effects of similarity and dissimilarity of stimuli and responses on learning, calls "convergent" and "divergent" hierarchy: "Where stimuli are varied and responses are functionally identical, positive transfer and retroactive facilitation are obtained, the magnitude of both increasing as the similarity among the stimulus members increases."[1] This is the convergent situation. The divergent hierarchy obtains in the following case: "Where stimuli are functionally identical and responses are varied, negative transfer and retroactive interference are obtained, the magnitude of both increasing as the stimulus similarity increases."

If we keep in mind that a class of affixes with grammatical function, whether prefixes or suffixes, has a small membership compared to that of the class of stems with

---

1. C. Osgood, "The Similarity Paradox in Human Learning: A Resolution," *Psychological Review*, LVI (1949), 132–43.

lexical meaning, then we may draw the parallel between prefixing, where a small class of affixes precedes a large class of stems, and the divergent hierarchy, in which a limited number of stimuli is followed by varied and divergent responses. The divergent hierarchy is marked by interference errors and slowness of response. The opposite situation obtains where the small class of suffixes follows the large root class. Here we have a large set of alternatives followed by a small class, a situation similar to the convergent paradigm of learning theory. Actually, these parallels are not exact, since the learning-theory situation involves stimuli followed by responses, while in speech we have a chaining of successive responses, although each response does involve self-stimulation, since the organism is aware of his own responses. Further, in the learning paradigm, each stimulus has a single "correct" response. For example, in the case of divergent hierarchy in which a series is interpolated with divergent responses, the subject first learns to respond to each particular stimulus with one response, e.g., stimulus s followed by response r_1. He then learns to respond to the *same* stimulus s followed by other divergent responses, r_2, r_3, etc., on the interpolated test. On retest to the first situation, there is interference from the interpolated material. In speech behavior there is no *one* correct root which follows a particular prefix. We have simply a small number of prefixes followed by a large number of roots, correctness of choice depending on the situationally appropriate meaning. The parallel is thus not exact, however suggestive. One may suggest a kind of experiment which would more closely parallel the speech situation. Let a large number of artificial objects, e.g., variously shaped and colored pieces of cardboard, be associated with nonsense terms. In addition, the subjects are to learn a small number of terms with relational meaning, such as "in front of you," "behind you," "to the right of you," etc. One group will be expected to react to phrases with the relational name preceding the object name by picking out the object and putting it in the appropriate position. The other will learn to react in the same fashion to the relational name *after* the object named. The first or prefix group will be expected to show greater latency of reaction (slowness) and a larger number of errors.

In addition to hierarchy, there are other relevant factors. One of these is the tendency toward anticipation observable in serial learning. There is a tendency to carry out responses appropriate at or near the goal before the organism has reached there, resulting in the short-circuiting of intermediate responses; there is little evidence of the opposite tendency to perseverate in earlier responses at a stage in the series where they are no longer appropriate. Similar factors evidently operate in linguistic behavior outside the prefix-suffix situation under discussion. In speech lapses it is far more frequently the features of some succeeding sound which effect the assimilation or dissimilation of an earlier sound by anticipation than the other way around. In regular conditioned sound changes, the conditioning factor is far more frequently a sound which follows than one which precedes. For example, the umlauting changes in Germanic languages involve an anticipatory fronting of a vowel in a preceding syllable when the following syllable has an i, and in the development of Italian from Latin, *octō*, "eight," has become *otto*. The factor of anticipation in its relation to prefixing and suffixing affects the stability rather than the genesis of the two techniques. The prefix which precedes the root will tend to be modified or completely suppressed by anticipation. Through sound changes, originally distinct prefixes will become merged. On the other hand, when the root is followed by a suffix, we shall expect the suffix in general to remain stable while the root develops irregularities.

A third factor has to do with the relative "importance" of the meaning conveyed by the root and the affix, a difference suggested by the traditional Chinese terminology in which roots are called "full words" and affixes "empty" words. This can be restated in terms of information theory. Since affix classes are small in membership compared to root classes, to make a choice among the members of an affix class eliminates far fewer of the possible sentences of the language as possibilities. Hence both in the technical sense of information theory and in the non-technical meaning of information, the utterance of a member of a root class of morphemes gives more information. One would hypothesize that the speaker will tend to choose that order which will, by giving the maximum information elements first, orient the hearer to the appropriate reactive behavior as soon as possible. The influence of the hearer or decoder who wishes to be oriented might be expected to be even more decisive. This factor will work against prefixes and in favor of suffixes. It is significant that apparently nowhere are noun case inflections prefixed to the noun stem. Case inflections are always insignificant in number compared to the membership of the root and stem classes. Imagine, for example, a Latin sentence in which the inflectional elements preceded the stems. Instead of *Petr-us Paul-um vĭd-et*, "Peter sees Paul," we might have *us-Petr um-Paul et-vĭd*. One can fairly hear the listener begging the speaker to get on with the business in hand!

Finally, there may be cited a fourth psychological factor, which, for want of an established term, will be called "vividness." In contrast to the information factor just mentioned, vividness refers chiefly to the reaction of the speaker or encoder rather than to the hearer or decoder. Certain aspects of the situation are the center of emotional or practical interest for the speaker and will tend to be elicited first. Probably all languages have methods by which normal word order can be reversed to allow for this. Adjectives are a word class which exhibits this factor of vividness. One would presumably not choose to use an adjective unless it made some emotional or practical difference: "that was a *beautiful* performance," "he lives in a *small* house," etc. In the case of adjective-noun order there is a tension between the demands of vividness on the speaker and of information on the hearer. The adjective class is smaller and gives less information. This conflict is reflected in the absence of any predominant linguistic rule for this construction. One solution arrived at again and again by languages is to have demonstratives, possessives, and (frequently) numerals, word groups whose vividness is particularly great, precede while other adjectives follow. This is the rule, for example, in substantially the same form in Romance languages and a whole series of languages, not all genetically related, in the Central Sudan.

The factor of vividness also works against prefixing, since affixes are presumably vested with a minimum of vividness compared to any root-stem class and hence will tend to follow rather than precede.

Some or all of these factors in combination also suggest a certain typical historical line of development. Once prefixes are established, the mechanism of various assimilative changes based on anticipation will result in what was originally a prefix, with a single fixed form, assuming various special alternants, depending on the phonemes of the following stem. For example, in Latin an original prefix *ad-* assimilates by anticipation its *-d-* to the initial consonant of the following stem (*ad + petō > appetō; ad + tineō > attineō; ad + cūsō > accūsō*, etc.). On the basis of divergent hierarchy, this development reduces the divergence by decreasing the variety of the responses to each stimulus. Now, given *ap-*, the divergence is limited to the much smaller following class of verb stems beginning with *p* rather than the entire class of verb stems which may follow *ad*. Likewise, from the point of view of information theory, such forms as *ap-, ac-, at-*, give more information than the single form *ad-*. Having chosen *ap-*, we have already reduced our choice among the possible following verb stems, so that a step has been taken in the direction of giving more information earlier in the utterance.

The continuance of this line of development leads more and more to special variants of the prefix, which narrows the choice of the following stem still further and in effect tends to make the choice of prefix and stem a psychologically single choice and descriptively a single unit. The climax of this development leads logically to an isolating form of speech in which the former prefixes have all been absorbed.

It is striking, but still tentative and incomplete, evidence that all the five isolating languages or language groups with which I have some acquaintance are genetically related to prefixing languages and that normal linguistic reconstruction in each case suggests that the prefixes are, in the main, original. The examples are Zapotec in the Oto-Mangue family of Mexico and Central America; Ewe in West Africa, which belongs to a nominal prefixing branch of the Niger-Congo family; Chinese and others in the Sino-Tibetan family; Thai in the Thai-Kadai-Indonesian family; and Annamite in the Austroasiatic family. The last two groups of languages illustrate another aspect of the problem. Along with prefixing, both have the device of infixing. One of the types of anticipation of a following root is to pronounce its initial phoneme before the prefix is finished (short-circuiting) and then compensate by pronouncing the rest of the prefix. The thesis that the relatively rare process of infixing usually grows out of prefixing seems to accord with general observation but is certainly in need of further systematic study. The Austroasiatic family illustrates a still further possibility. The Munda languages of this family, instead of developing in the direction of isolation, have tended more and more to build up new suffix constructions, so that suffixing is now dominant over the obsolescent technique of prefixing.

One may tentatively suggest the following typological sequence, starting with isolating languages. An isolating language may develop into either a predominantly prefixing or predominantly suffixing one, the latter far more frequently. A prefixing language tends either to isolation (e.g., Annamite) or to suffixing (e.g., Munda), probably more often the latter. A suffixing language cannot become a prefixing language, certainly not directly. Suffixing tends to persist, but suffixing languages can move toward isolation just as prefixing languages do. However, a predominantly suffixing language which has moved in the direction of isolation (i.e., has become quite analytic), like English or Persian, presents a quite different aspect from a fully isolating language which has arisen from a prefixing language.

It was noted earlier that the factor of anticipation would tend to modify a stem which precedes a suffix. Parallel to the line of development sketched for prefixing languages, this results, from the point of view of information theory, in the reduction of the amount of information given by the suffix, since the choice of a particular root modification narrows down the choice of possible suffixes. This is typical for many suffixing languages, with their numerous and irregular declensional and conjugational classes. As the suffixes give less information, they in turn become largely superfluous and are reduced or lost, the difference in function now being carried by alternations of the root. Hence internal change, Sapir's symbolism, is characteristic of suffixing languages which are moving toward isolation.

The development of the singular-plural alternation of the type *foot*:*feet* in English will illustrate this process. The difference was originally carried by suffixes. The characteristic mechanism of anticipation resulted in umlauting of the original internal $\bar{o}$ vowel of the root *fōt-* through fronting to $\ddot{o}$, and unrounding to *e-*, preceding the front vowel *i* which marked the plural (*fōti* > *föti* > *fēti*). Through this development, the plural distinction was carried by both the final *i* and the vowel contrast of the root: singular *fōt*, plural *fēti*. Since the choice of *fēt-* over *fōt* already involved a choice of *-i*, this *-i* was redundant. It gave no information in the technical sense, since it did not reduce the number of alternatives. It was then dropped, leaving internal change as the sole mechanism of distinguishing number.

A typical example of this kind of development on a broad scale is offered by such Nilotic languages as Shilluk and Nuer, which express practically all relational meanings by intricate and highly irregular internal changes. These languages are most closely related to the Great Lakes group, including Masai, Bari, Nandi, Lotuko, and Turkana. These latter languages are strongly suffixing, with numerous irregular formations. Similar mechanisms of change described previously for English can be traced here. Anticipation of the quality of final vowels and complex tonal glides, the latter part of which arose from anticipation of the tonal level of the original suffix, play a prominent role. As in English, but far less frequently, there are still surviving suffix formations, for example, a nominal plural in *-i* in Shilluk.

The theses regarding the order of affixed elements advanced here, exploratory as they are, will help to illustrate some types of universals with which a general linguistics can deal. It is obvious that much remains to be done both in the accumulation of descriptive and historical knowledge and in the codification and archiving of existing linguistic information before we can proceed with greater confidence. It should also be clear from the present discussion that the explanation of linguistic universals necessarily brings in non-linguistic considerations, including the psychological factors which are generally reckoned to be on a different and lower level than the cultural facts of which linguistic facts are a part. In this way we pass beyond the purely descriptive generalizations which constitute the traditional linguistic explanations. However tentatively in the present instance, numbers of different universal facts about language are tied into the same causal network as deductive consequences of certain psychological facts. This does not mean that the traditional "superorganic" approach of linguistics is unjustified. Before we can arrive at universals, each specific case must be understood as far as possible in terms of its specific historic antecedents and its specific synchronic concomitants. Otherwise we fall prey to the *ad hoc* use of generalizations, often tautological, adduced to explain some specific linguistic fact without regard to its descriptive and historical context. It is this type of explanation, sometimes offered by psychologists, which has made the linguist justifiably suspicious of passing beyond the facts of his own level.

Of course, psychology does not by itself provide a total explanation. This is shown conclusively enough by the fact that the same general principles of human behavior at work on the same initial linguistic structure never produce the same end result. Related languages are always different. As illustrated by the present instance, we arrive only at lesser and greater probabilities, which may eventually be quantified. Prefixing as a mechanism is less frequently chosen than suffixing. But why one choice is made in one case and a different one in another still eludes us. In addition to principles of individual behavior, there are, of course, relevant considerations based on social and cultural factors. For example, the profound effect often exerted on a language by another language cannot be understood without taking into account the general frame of cultural contact and societal interrelations. With all these we are nearer our goal, but not yet arrived. A full understanding of linguistic phenomena requires consideration of both intra-linguistic and extra-linguistic factors some of which are at present but imperfectly understood; others there must be whose nature we cannot at present even guess.

ON BASIC RELATIONS IN SIGN SYSTEMS

As stated in the text, we usually think of a sign system as having a single serial relation as a basic requirement; for example, the relation "following in time" in speech and "immediately to the right" in written English. Other relations are either additional serial relations or equivalence relations. Examples of equivalence relations are equality in arithmetic or similarity in color in everyday language. An equivalence relation is reflexive (for all x it holds between x and x), symmetrical (if it holds between x and y, it holds between y and x), and transitive (if it holds between x and y and between y and z, it holds between x and z). Serial relations, by contrast, are irreflexive, asymmetrical, and transitive. A typical equivalence relation in sign systems is simultaneity of sound features, and the existence of such equivalence relations in addition to serial relations is typical of sound as a medium for sign systems as opposed to visual representations. An example is the pitch of a vowel which is simultaneous with its quality.

The relation "above" as with written accents in language or the dash over a variable p indicating "not-p" are examples of additional serial relations. In these examples there is a maximum, two, to the number of elements forming the series generated by the additional relation. This is not a necessary restriction. It is possible to have two-dimensional blocks without maxima in either direction. For that matter, we can construct three-dimensional systems in specified visual systems and abstract systems of any number of dimensions, though we may not wish to include systems with more than one serial relation without sequences of maximum length in our definition of sign system.

All such systems can be reduced to, that is, rendered isomorphic with, a system containing only one serial relation. For n such relations we specify for each element n co-ordinates and then arrange the indexes in numerical order. The elements can then be arranged in a single line, i.e., by a single serial relation, by ordering them according to their co-ordinates. Where necessary, an additional symbol will indicate a blank position. Thus, in the following two-dimensional array, the co-ordinates of n are $(1, 1)$, of s $(3, 2)$:

$$\begin{vmatrix} a & k & r \\ x & t & s \\ n & u & v \end{vmatrix}.$$

This can be written as: $a\,x\,n\,k\,t\,u\,r\,s\,v$.

In the same way, in symbolic language $\bar{p}$, "not -p," is also written $\sim p$. Similarly, simultaneous elements can be reduced to a single serial relation. One method is a consistent, but arbitrary, assignment of position, as in written English, where the question intonation simultaneous with the sentence is written after it. Another method is for each combination of simultaneous components, where the system is of finite order, to be considered a new element and assigned a separate symbol. This occurs in alphabetic writing considered as an isomorphic representation of the components of spoken language. Many problems which have plagued phonemic theorists arise simply from the fact that phonemics involves a visual medium with characteristically serial relations, as opposed to the equivalence relations inherent in the sound medium.

The fundamental position of a single serial relation consists, then, in the fact that, without at least one such relation, we would not say that we had a sign system. On the other hand, systems with additional relations, whether serial or equivalence, can be rendered isomorphic to some system with a single serial relation.

APPENDIX II

ON ORDINAL RULES

Ordinal rules can be stated as functions whose set of arguments is the natural numbers. All other rules can then be stated as ordinal rules, that is, by means of such functions. This can be accomplished as follows: First, as in the text discussion of ordinal rules, an order is established among all the possible expressions made up from the elements. Another way of stating this is to say that the expressions of the infinite language homogeneous to the one we are describing have been placed in one-to-one correspondence with the natural numbers. A complete grammar, then, is one which assigns to each natural number n as argument either the value 1 if the nth expression belongs in the language or 0 if it does not.

If, for example, we have a sign system with three elements specified as a, b, and c and we assign them this order and if we have as our sole grammatical rule that a may not immediately follow a, then the expressions of I_3 thus specified are as follows, together with their numeral arguments among the natural numbers:

$a, 1$; $b, 2$; $c, 3$; $aa, 4$; $ab, 5$; $ac, 6$; $ba, 7$; $bb, 8$; $bc, 9$; $ca, 10$; $cb, 11$; $cc, 12$; $aaa, 13$; $aab, 14$; $aac, 15$; etc.

Then $f(1) = 1$; $f(2) = 1$; $f(3) = 1$; $f(4) = 0$; $f(8) = 1$; $f(13) = 0$ are examples of the values of this function, since expressions 4 and 13 involve a forbidden sequence aa and the others do not.

The same function may be expressed by a dyadic fraction as follows: 0.1110111111110001 . . . , where there are zeros in the fourth, thirteenth, fourteenth, and fifteenth places.

Since, by definition, any sign system is different from another if at least one expression is different, it follows that to every real number between 0 and 1 there corresponds a sign system. For example, $\sqrt{2}$ states the grammar of a sign system. To $0 = 0.00000 \ldots$, there corresponds the null language, and to $1 = 0.1111111 \ldots$, the infinite language. The number of possible homogeneous sign systems of the same order can thus be brought into one-to-one relation with the continuum and is uncountable.

To every finite language with expressions of maximum length l, there corresponds a rational fraction between 0 and 1. To every non-maximal language of infinite order, there corresponds an infinite set of sequences of natural numbers, i.e., an expression of order type ω^2. To every SS of infinite order but with expressions of maximal length l, there corresponds an expression of order type $l\omega$.

THE EXTERNAL TRANSFORMATION OF SIGN
SYSTEMS

In the text, only element-for-element substitution isomorphisms were considered. Other isomorphisms can be obtained by which, to each expression of one SS, an expression of another SS can be made to correspond, indicating a likeness of structure in the two SS's. Still using substitution but making a sequence of elements in one system correspond to a single element in the other, an isomorphism between a system with sequences as units and the corresponding system with the "same grammar" but elements as units can be specified. This relation holds between the "same" language written alphabetically and ideographically. Similarly, a syllabic isomorphism can exist, as in syllabic writing and alphabetic writing of the same language.

Another method of generating isomorphisms is by transposition, i.e., changes of position. If we take the final element or final sequence or a specific number of elements or sequences and transfer them from the end of each expression to the beginning, then each of the expressions of the old system is connected with those of the new by a transposition transformation. The inverse transformation, by which elements at the beginning are transferred to the end, carries each expression of the new system back into one of the original system. Such transformations may be compounded, e.g., the result of transferring three elements and then two is the same as transferring five. They therefore form a free cyclic group. The set of element-for-element substitution transformations likewise forms a group, the symmetric group of group theory.

Another method of obtaining isomorphisms involves multiplication of sets. If M and N are sets, then the product set $M \times N$ consists of any expression of M followed by any expression of N. The number of expressions of $M \times N$ will be the numerical product of the number of expressions in the two factor systems. It is clear that $M \times N$ is not, in general, the same set as $N \times M$. Isomorphisms arise only in this way through multiplication of any system, finite or infinite, by a finite SS which contains only a single expression. If L_1 is any SS and L_2 has only the expression $\{acd\}$, then $L_1 \times L_2$ consists of every expression of L_1 followed by $\{acd\}$. The inverse transformation, by removing ("dividing by") $\{acd\}$, carries every expression of $L_1 \times L_2$ into the corresponding expression of L_1.

The applicability of set multiplication is mainly where both factors are finite systems. If we form a finite language out of all the stems of some word class in a language, then the effect of adding a suffix is obtained by multiplication of this finite language by a language in which the suffix is the only expression. In prefixing, the order of factors is reversed. The reduplicated forms are a sublanguage (the so-called main diagonal) of the finite language multiplied by itself, that is, squared.

To allow for infixing and, in general, for isomorphisms in which a single element or sequence of elements is inserted within, rather than put before or after, the expressions of another language, the usual theory of sets would have to be extended.

Such operations as multiplication by some particular finite system, whether this system has one or more than one expression, provide a rule by which any SS can be transformed into some other SS, even if not isomorphically. This suggests extending the notion of function to entire sign systems. The function $\times\{acd\}$ assigns to any system as argument a different system as its value. This is also true of the complement operation, which is a one-to-one function, which assigns to any SS the homogeneous system of the same order made up of all the expressions which it does not itself contain.

GLOSSARY OF DEFINITIONS IN CHAPTER I

ABSTRACT SYSTEM—A sign system in which the physical objects which are to function as elements have not been specified.

AMBIGUOUS SUBCONSTRUCTION—A subconstruction which contains one or more expressions which belong to another subconstruction.

ANALYTIC OPERATION—An operation by means of which, given a sample of the expressions of a particular sign system, rules are deduced.

BASIC CLASS OF A CONSTRUCTION—A class which appears in every subconstruction.

BASIS OF A CONSTRUCTION—The subconstruction of smallest length.

CALCULUS—A sign system without rules of meaning.

CARDINAL RULE—Rules which concern the cardinal number of occurrences of a particular unit in a sign system.

CONSTRUCTION—A class of subconstructions derived from a basis by rules of vertical transformation.

CONSTRUCTIONAL PARTITION—The division of the expression of a sign system such that each is assigned to one of a finite number of constructions. The constructions are not necessarily mutually exclusive.

CONTEXTUAL CLASS—A class of units consisting of some particular unit in an expression together with all those other units, if any, which may replace the given unit to produce other valid expressions of the sign system.

DEFINITE TRANSITION—A rule of definite transition requires that, at some definite interval before or after a given unit, some other unit is required or excluded.

ELEMENT ORDER—The number of elements in a sign system.

EQUALITY OF SIGN SYSTEMS—Two sign systems are equal if they have the same expressions.

EXTENDED CLASS—A class of units consisting of some particular unit of an expression, together with all those other units which appear in the same position through a chain of horizontal transformations.

FINITE SIGN SYSTEM—A sign system with a finite number of expressions.

GRAMMATICAL ASPECT—That aspect of a sign system which concerns the permitted combinations of elements in expressions which belong to the system.

HETEROGENEOUS SIGN SYSTEMS—Two specified sign systems are heterogeneous either if they are of the same element order and do not have the same signs or if they are of different order and the sign system of lower order has at least one sign which is not in the system of higher order.

HETEROGENEOUS SUBCONSTRUCTION—A subconstruction in which not all the classes have the same membership.

HOMOGENEOUS SIGN SYSTEMS—Two specified sign systems are homogeneous either if they are of the same element order and have the same signs or if they are of different order and every sign of the system of lower order is a sign of the system of higher order.

HOMOGENEOUS SUBCONSTRUCTION—A subconstruction in which all the classes have the same membership.

HORIZONTAL TRANSFORMATION—One expression of a sign system is a horizontal transformation of another if it can be obtained from it by replacing some unit of the expression by another unit of the same kind.

IMPERFECT SUBCONSTRUCTION—An imperfect subconstruction is one in which not all expressions made up of sequences involving members of the succession of classes are part of the system.

INDEFINITE TRANSITION—A rule of indefinite transition requires that a certain unit cannot or must be preceded or followed by some other particular unit without the interval between them being specified.

INFINITE INTERPOLATION—A rule for constructing expressions from two or more different classes of elements such that there is a limit to the number of occurrences of one of the classes and no limit to the number of occurrences of at least one of the others.

INFINITE SIGN SYSTEM—A sign system with an infinite number of expressions.

INFINITE SIGN SYSTEM OF A GIVEN ORDER—The sign system of that order which contains all possible permutations and combinations of the element.

INTERPRETED SYSTEM—A sign system for which there are rules of meaning.

INTERSECTION OF SIGN SYSTEMS—A sign system which contains only those expressions which are contained in both of two sign systems is their intersection.

ISOMORPHISM—A relation between sign systems such that by rules of transformation each expression in one system corresponds to one expression in the other and vice versa.

LENGTH OF AN EXPRESSION—The number of units in an expression.

LINEAR CONSTRUCTION—A construction which contains only one subconstruction of each unit length.

MAXIMUM—A rule of maximum states that a particular unit may not have more than some fixed number of occurrences in any expression.

MINIMUM—A rule of minimum states that a particular unit must have at least some fixed number of occurrences in every expression.

MODIFICATION—A class X in a construction modifies a class Y if there are subconstructions which contain Y but not X but none which contain X without Y.

NEGATIVE TRANSITION—A rule of negative transition places some limitation on the occurrences of a particular unit in terms of some other unit.

NON-CONTEXTUAL CLASS—A class of units based on occurrence in a particular position in partial expressions compared without reference to the rest of the context in which they occur.

ORDER—The order of a system is the number of different units it contains.

ORDINAL RULE—A rule which includes or excludes certain expressions of a sign system on the basis of the position in which they appear in an ordering of all the expressions of the system.

PERFECT SUBCONSTRUCTION—A perfect subconstruction is one in which every expression made up of sequences involving members of the successive classes is part of the system.

PHYSICAL ASPECT—That aspect of a sign system which concerns the physical phenomena which are to be taken as instances of the elements and relations.

POSITIVE TRANSITION—A rule of positive transition is one which requires the occurrence of some particular unit in every expression in which some other particular unit occurs.

PRAGMATIC ASPECT—That aspect of a sign system which has to do with the behavior involved in its use.

RAMIFIED CONSTRUCTION—A construction which contains more than one subconstruction for certain lengths.

RESTRICTED CLASS—A class of units consisting of some particular unit in an expression, together with all those other units, if any, which may replace the given unit to produce other valid expressions of the sign, provided that, for all expressions obtained from the original by the addition or subtraction of units, there exist corresponding expressions in which the substituted member occurs and vice versa.

SEMANTIC ASPECT—That aspect of a sign system which concerns rules of meaning.

SEQUENCE—A succession of elements treated as a unit in the application and discovery of rules.

SEQUENCE ORDER—The number of different sequences in a sign system.

SERIAL RELATION—A relation among elements or sequences of an expression with the logical characteristics of the generating relation of a finite progression; i.e., there is a first and last member, and every member except the first has a single immediate predecessor and every member except the last a single immediate successor.

SPECIFIED SYSTEM—A system in which the physical phenomena to be considered as representations of the elements and relations have been specified.

SUBCONSTRUCTION—A set of expressions of given length defined as the members of a succession of classes.

SYNTHETIC OPERATION—An operation by which expressions of a sign system may be constructed by references to stated rules.

TRANSITION—A rule of transition is one which excludes or requires the occurrence of one particular unit of an expression in which some other particular unit occurs.

UNAMBIGUOUS SUBCONSTRUCTION—A subconstruction which does not contain any expression which is a member of another subconstruction.

UNION OF SIGN SYSTEMS—A sign system which contains all the expressions of two sign systems which are found in either or both is their union.

UNIT—Element or sequence.

VERTICAL TRANSFORMATION—A rule which assigns to each subconstruction or expression of length n one or more subconstructions or expressions, respectively, of next greater length, usually $n + 1$.

INDEX

PHOENIX BOOKS

PHOENIX BOOKS

PHOENIX BOOKS

 PHOENIX SCIENCE SERIES